Point of Art

by Robert Maniscalco

© 2007 by Robert Maniscalco.

© Second Edition 2013

Cover image:

Spring of '39, oil, 30" x 40" by Robert Maniscalco.

Published by PointOfArt

ISBN: 978-1478123545

1478123540

Printed in the United States of America

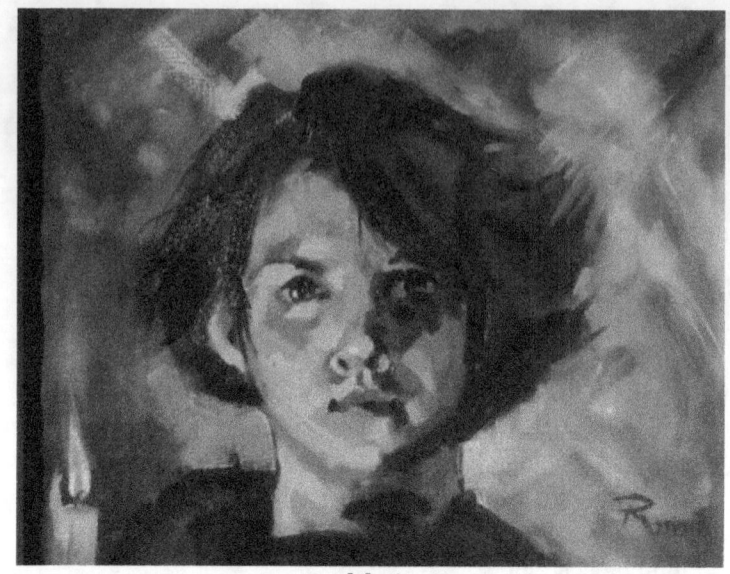

Marie

Dedicated to all my hardworking and talented

students, who, over the course of many years,

have taught me so much.

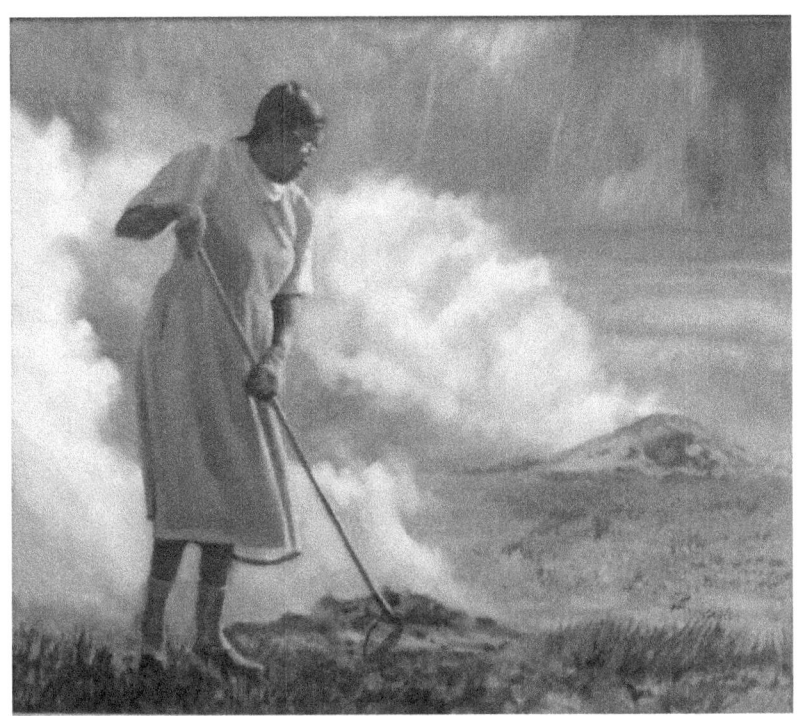

Fires of Wadmalaw

For more information go to: **www.maniscalcogallery.com**

Table of Contents

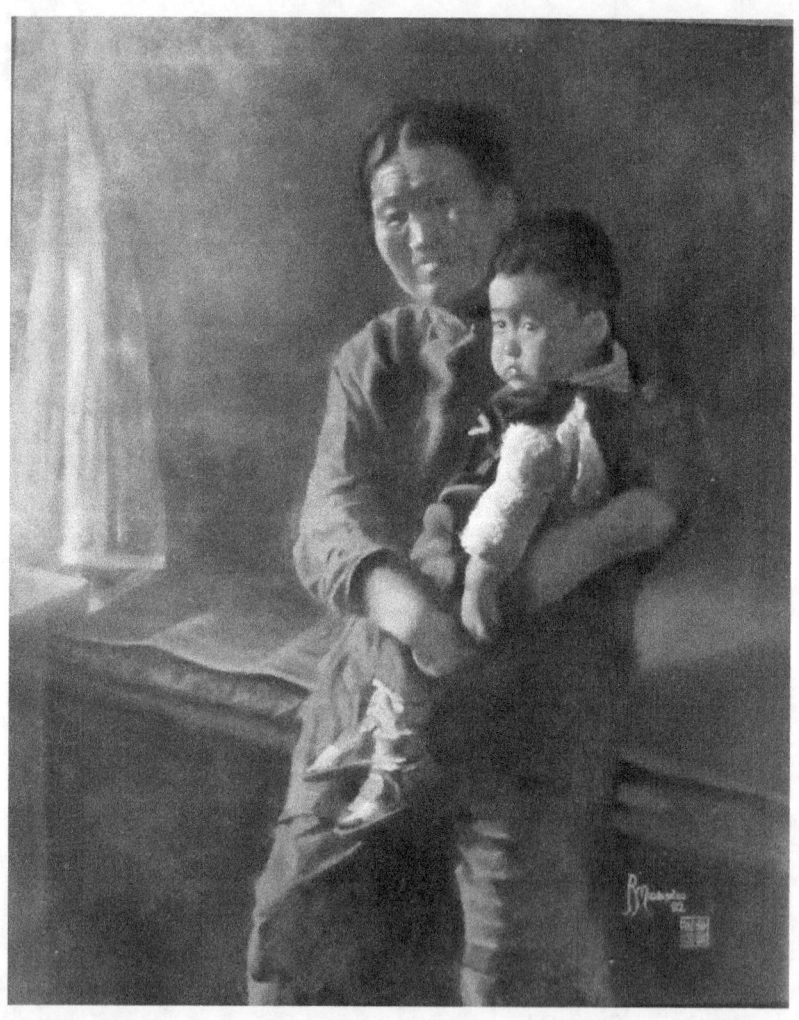

"The Old and the New"

Introduction by the Author

The ideas expressed in this book are not intended as any gospel of art. They are musings from my particular journey as an artist, arts advocate and teacher. They are meditations, intended to provide access to the creative process. Take them for what they're worth. If they open up possibilities for artistic growth then they will have served their humble purpose.

I should point out at the beginning that there is no one "right" way to do a thing, particularly in the realm of creativity. In the first section of this book I present a lot of rules, structures and advice, which are directed to the serious student of representational painting. But there are many other serious schools of painting where these rules simply don't apply. Much of what I've written speaks to these schools as well. Some of my coaching may seem quite logical while at other times it may seem counter-intuitive. You may disagree with some—or all—of what I say in these pages. That is as it should be. The truth is revealed in the myriad of controversy. My intention, nonetheless, is to honor all creative self-expression in a non-judgmental way.

ROBERT MANISCALCO

Many people have said to me over the years, "I envy you. I can't even draw a straight line." It breaks my heart to know that many people have grown into adulthood convinced they cannot draw. Drawing, painting and creativity are not magical gifts for a chosen few. I'm convinced that everyone can learn how to communicate with pictures; we're all entitled to some measure of visual literacy. It's a natural human attribute. This book is intended to move us a little closer to the ever-elusive creative epiphany— those rare glimpses of ecstasy and clarity when we become lost in the non-verbal, serene place of the creative mind.

This book consists of two sections. The first part is a series of short, randomly arranged insights and ideas ranging between practical advice on painting to finding the most effective mind-set for working as a professional artist. They are what one might hear from me in a class or workshop. The second part is a series of essays dealing with a variety of larger arts issues. They consist mostly of excerpts from a monthly column I wrote for the Pointer Magazine in Grosse Pointe, Michigan. The "Pointe of Art" column ran from 2001 to 2005 and focused on arts topics, often specific to the Detroit area. The themes addressed, however, are universal. There are a number of essays about the profession of being an artist, which may be of benefit to those considering a career as an artist. Several sections deal with advocacy issues. I make no apology about repetition. Often, ideas are expressed from different angles to drive home each point.

These musings and essays are not intended in any order or sequence. I encourage you to open this book to any page and find the message that speaks to you at that moment, rather than read it cover to cover.

POINT OF ART

Finally, you may notice the conspicuous absence of illustrations, which may seem odd for a book about art. My intention is to ask the reader to visualize or conjure the concepts in his/her mind rather than make a passing glance at illustrations or charts. Visual aids, such as color charts, etc. are available on my website: www.maniscalcogallery.com.

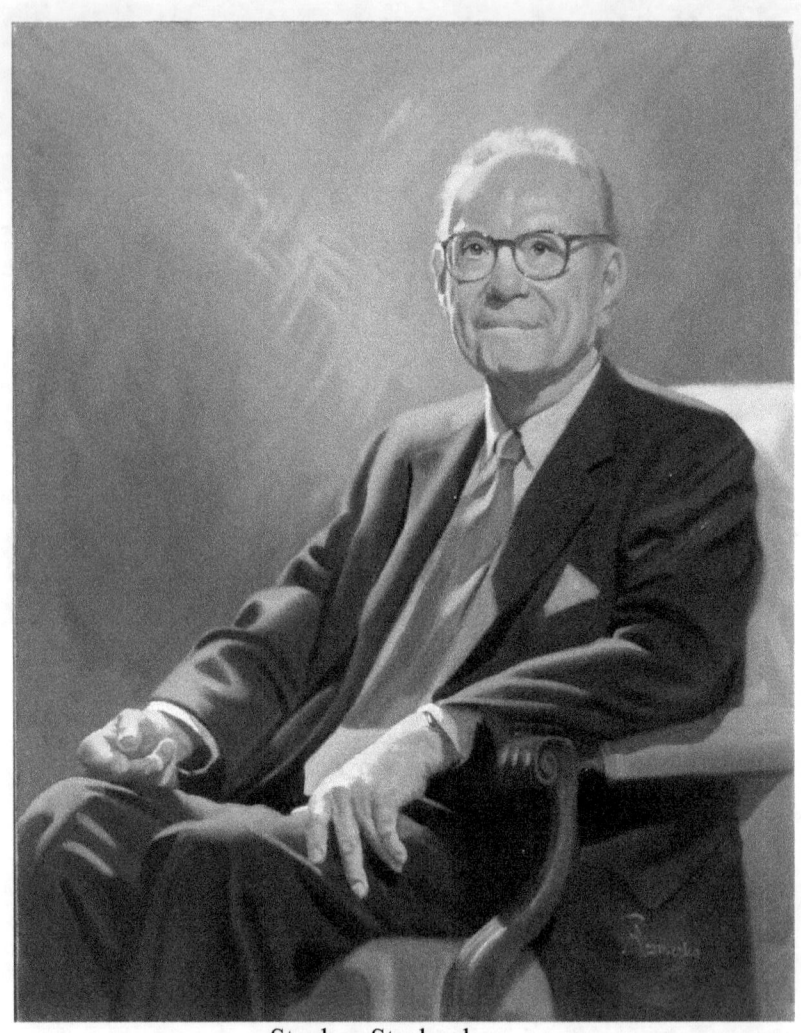

Stephan Stackpole

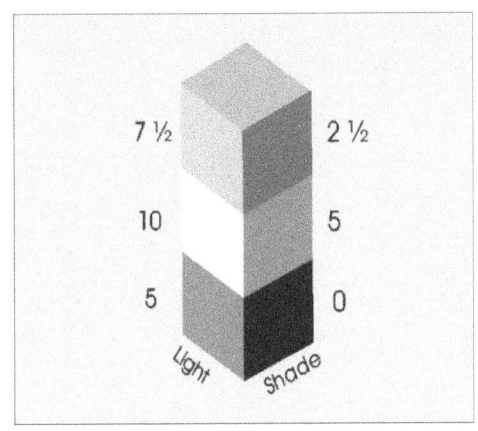

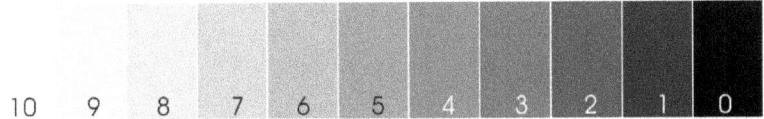

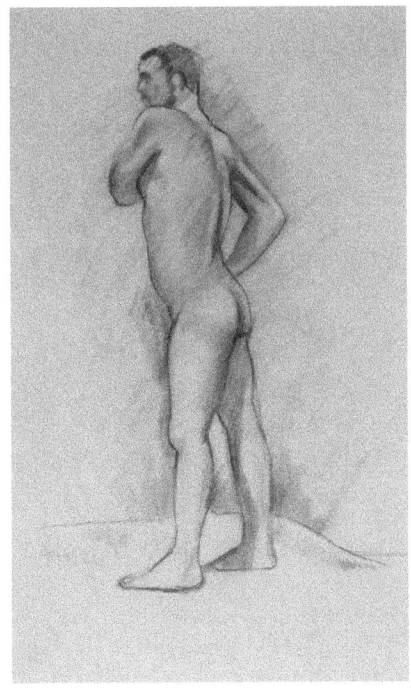

Point of Art:

Part 1

The Teacher's Muse—
Insights and Ideas

The true artist has a point of view but recognizes beauty in all its forms. His world-view is unlimited.

Art and nature are full of contradictions. Look for the yin and yang: hard and soft, dark and light, red and green. Relating and juxtaposing "opposites" helps to achieve balance. They are the building blocks of structure.

God is not a mechanical being. Nature presents a certain complexity that we are challenged to express. Art is about honoring the specific randomness of form. Avoid repetitive patterns.

On the other hand, there are lines that are not drawn, but visualized, that connect forms to one another. It's amazing how many of these linear relationships there are in the seeming chaos of nature. These "imaginary" lines hold all the complexities together.

Sad as it may be, most people will never make the effort to understand art. Without some understanding of the language of art they will likely never learn to appreciate it. We must not let this stop us.

You may want to fool around with that drawing or you might just want to let it happen in the paint. It's up to you.

Start with the overall value. Get the mass shapes and then break them up into darks and lights. Find the largest shapes first.

Don't be afraid to continually return to what's most important: the large masses.

What is your style, your vision? Style has everything to do with your particular choices. What will you include and what will you exclude from your field of vision? What is most essential to the painting? Paint what's most important to you.   This is your style.

When painting, think of forms as solid masses abutting one another rather than as a series of lines. Use visualized lines to relate forms to one another but paint the masses.

There are perfectly balanced compositions, which are sometimes so perfect they're boring. And then there are those compositions that intentionally force the viewer into another place, another view, an uncomfortable place. It is a bit more eccentric perhaps. It says something about the subject, something about the artist. It makes us think.

Does one really have to be in the mood to do what he or she loves? Absolutely. Getting in the mood is an art in itself. One's ability to create the proper mood is what separates the novice from the professional.

Representational painting is about values. When you can master increments of value like a musician masters scales, then you can paint anything you see.

After solid painting skills, a love of people is a prerequisite for doing portraits.

It's really a matter of reconciling our left and right brains. We need to find a healthy balance.

Whether you are painting realistically or not, it is beneficial to begin to see shapes and patterns abstractly.

It's about learning how to see and interpret nature in a way that allows us to paint expressively. It's a different way of seeing.

It's more objective than subjective. It depends more upon choosing from what we actually see rather than what we think we see or should be seeing. The premise is simple: sight leads to insight.

In direct sunlight or under a modeling light, black in the light is the same value as white in the shadow.

The fact that black in the light is the same value as white in the shadow might say something about race relations. I'm not sure what.

God was very good to artists, creating forms in nature, which are related so beautifully one to another. Our job is to delicately unwrap these mysteries like a child opening a birthday present—ripping and tearing with the urgency of a child discovering the next toy.

I can't tell you how many artists have walked through my gallery door, their eyes staring at the floor, arms full of artwork, bragging that they've never looked at anyone else's work, that their work is completely original. My point is this: artwork created in a vacuum tends to be lacking a connection to humanity. It's rarely ever original.

In any discipline of endeavor it is essential to agree upon the jargon (the language used to express the essential concepts), to avoid confusion.

In order to use color effectively we must understand its various components. Value-based painting means we are emphasizing the lightness or darkness of color over the other elements (hue and chroma). In other words, we are not distracting ourselves with vague, poetic descriptions of color like "beige", "scarlet", "puce," or terms like "bright orange," which are very subjective.

Some artists, after years of careful observation, come to understand values intuitively. But for most, it is an acquired skill.

One of the most important things God did in creation was divide the night from the day. We need to follow His example by understanding how to segregate those areas receiving direct light from those in the shadow.

We live in a hue based society. When we refer to a color it's always in relation to hue. "There's a red fire truck." "The sky is so blue today." We use hue to survive from childhood. We learn to stop at a red light and go when it's green. When we, as artists, are able to get off this preconditioned response to hue and concentrate on value, it will free up our creative use of hue.

Confusion is the only state in which new things are possible. During states of heightened awareness and control we will only do well what has already ever been done before. Without confusion there is no inquiry. Without inquiry there is no innovation. My best ideas come when I misunderstand another's idea. It was my sweet Mary, who spends much of her time not knowing what day it is or what planet she's on, who said, "my tears are afraid of love." A line I find extremely beautiful and meaningful. She is completely present in the now. As an artist I believe it is my job to create and cultivate confusion so that amazing things will happen, as if to fill the void confusion brings into being. Improvisation, splatter painting, random thoughts juxtaposed to create something new. This is the artistic impulse.

Ever notice how most people talk about how excited they are by the new artwork they've acquired and how well it goes in their decor. Artists talk about the new sofa and how well it will match all the art s/he is making.

As an experiment, my wife Cate blasted Gustav Mahler at a high end eyewear store in the posh retail area of Charleston, where she works part time. She noted a 500% increase in sales.

The intuition of a genius is of more value than the intuition of a Trogladyte, unless you are trying to survive in a cave.

There is cleverness in Desire.

If you have the option of doing anything it is highly likely you will do nothing.

Sometimes we have to decide between beauty and perfection. We train for control so we can give it up, throw it aside, addept that it is not meant to be. Control is not a means to an end. If it was we'd end up with the dull, mechanical sterility of perfection. We can't afford to lose our sould in the quest for perfection.

Painters have more in common with magicians than with detectives.

Our job as artists is to express how our subject departs from the norm, not how it conforms.

Painting in a vacuum sucks!

Edges trump texture. Shapes trump edges. Value trumps shapes. Awesome trumps value.

When is stating the obvious also a statement of truth?

Are artists playing God or they merely agents of God?

Trying something new without truly having an open mind is just mental masterbation.

It helps to consider shadows as "things."

The envelope can also be thought of as a nutshell, as in "that's it in a nutshell."

Follow your heart when it comes to hue. Follow your mind when it comes to value.

POINT OF ART

We need to develop our ability to translate colors into value. Most representational artists know how to do this. They know it's all about manipulating a scale of values, even though they'd rather talk about hue. After all, it's much more glamorous to talk about the golden glow of the autumn sun than to discuss its relative value.

When we focus on values, and hue takes a back seat, we are much more likely to combine hues in unusual, original ways. We do this subconsciously; hues are not of primary concern to us. We are focusing our conscious mind on values.

Any color we see in nature can be boiled down to some combination of the primary and secondary hues. Any hue we see can also be broken down as having a particular value and chroma. We need to train our eye by isolating these components.

One thing you might take a moment to do is to write the actual values of the color directly onto your tubes of paint so you know what you're getting into when you put the color out on your palette.

Once you assimilate a piece of information you don't have to remember it. This takes more time than memorization.

Anything that's complicated must be simplified. Anything that's simple must be specific. Anything that's specific must be true.

The beauty in the Power Palette is in its subtle color relationships. Add neutral gray to yellow and you can get the most exquisite green. Add red to neutral and you'll get an amazingly subtle purple. All color combinations in the Power Palette are completely harmonious. You can view the Power Palette on my website. Go to: www.maniscalcogallery.com.

As you add white to a color it will become lighter, but drop in chroma. That is called tinting.

Likeness depends primarily on two things, excellent drawing and an accurate description of form, which has everything to do with values.

Drawing is the parent, painting the child!

Failure is only possible when you've stopped trying.

What is it we actually do when we draw? The basic principles of drawing are not as difficult as they may seem. The key idea is to relate forms to one another. Once you have the concept that everything is relative, the process will become second nature.

Here's a great exercise you can do with the morning paper: using any photo you like, draw as many straight lines connecting as many points as possible (if you can't draw a straight line, use a ruler!!). You'll be amazed at how many points are related along straight lines. These are called linear relationships.

The envelope is the essential expression of every shape. Think of it as cutting and folding a customized envelope into which you could literally insert the shape. It's a series of straight lines at specific angles, which envelop the unique shape. Deciding which points are most important and calculating the specific angles between these points is crucial in determining an accurate envelope.

POINT OF ART

All shapes, down to the smallest cells, have a specific envelope.

There's a balance in drawing between what I call the "three Rs." They are relative negative/positive shapes, relative lines (or linear relationships) and relative measurements (or proportions).

When there are discrepancies between the negative/positive shapes we observe in our subject and those in our drawing it is a good indication that the proportions or linear relationships need attention. They are each interrelated. When something is wrong with the proportions, for instance, there's a good chance that a linear relationship or negative/positive shape is also off. Assess the situation by isolating these various components and you will be able to resolve any drawing issue.

For portraits, I like to measure the largest proportion first by comparing the widest part of the head (usually at eye level) with the tallest part (usually from the top of the head to x—i.e. the bottom of the nose or the mouth). From there I can build out the larger masses like shadow patterns, forehead, eye sockets, etc. I don't think about drawing features like eyes, mouths, etc until much later in the process, if at all.

Remember, being specific and accurate doesn't necessarily have anything to do with finish or detail.

Don't confuse "style" with a lack of skill. One must master the rudiments, as a musician masters his instrument, before something called style can emerge.

As a painter we are concentrating on form. Therefore it is important to point out that when two forms come in contact with one another they create the illusion of a line, when in reality there are no outlines/contours in nature. Lines are an invention of the artist.

Avoid blending early on. And then, be selective.

There are many ways to paint a straight line. One way is with a fine round brush, used like a pencil. Another is to turn a wide flat brush on its side and insert a line. A slightly more jagged, and consequently more expressive and sensitive line will result.

Let the egg shape of the head grow towards its "outline," rather than drawing an outline and filling it in. This may not fit into our coloring book, cookie-cutter mentality we carry from childhood but it makes sense for painting form.

It is wise to avoid symmetry or cutting a rectangle in half.

Avoid making the distances from the edge of the picture plane and the subject equal. Don't place the focal point dead center.

If the subject is centered make sure the surrounding areas are broken up to create spatial variety.

Try to achieve variety when it comes to choosing exit points.

There should always be a path leading the eye into the picture and directing it to the focal point.

It may help to think of shadows as thing, as important as eyes, noses and mouths.

Leaving is the first and most important step to returning.

The more lines (linear relationships) running through the image the more unified it will become.

Look for triangles in your designs.

On the other hand, when I scan over a nearly finished painting, one thing I look for are small sharp triangles that grab for my eye's attention.

Usually they are in competition with the focal point of the painting. I like to soften these sharp edges to allow my eye to pass over them.

Light and dark masses should be arranged in a composition to create interesting and expressive abstract shapes.

Masses should never abut other masses, including the picture plane. Rather they should overlap whenever possible.

Keep in mind we can spend a lifetime learning the basic principles but the best way to learn is to apply new information as you go, one painting at a time. Each painting poses special challenges, which require special solutions.

There are basically two ways to proceed with the painting. One way is to do an accurate line drawing first with charcoal or the brush, perhaps with burnt umber. The other way is to start with large painted masses, which can be broken down (drawn) into smaller and smaller shapes, each having a particular value. Both require excellent drawing skills and an understanding of values.

Working from a photograph requires an understanding of how nature behaves, which requires the experience and knowledge of working from life.

ROBERT MANISCALCO

The transparent effect of an under-painting is not only practical it can add real depth to the finished work. There is a whole dimension of textures and "air" effects achievable with a good under-painting, which can be left in the finished work.

Check out Rembrandt. He used under-paintings to great effect. The beauty of it is this: transparent colors can be treated like watercolors, with similar results. It is possible to build up multiple transparent glazes to create wonderful vibrations of color.

Should we paint the forest or the trees? Ignore the "leaves," the small details, for now.

Back in the '60s they used to say, "everything is relative." It's still true today.

The right-brain is non-verbal. Language, and consequently the go, resides on the left-brain. Both sides are creative in their own way.

Painting and drawing are activities of the right-brain. But the right-brain needs gentle prompting from the left-brain to stay on task. Don't let the loud-mouthed left-brain trample on the defenseless right-brain. The right-brain freezes when the left-brain's ego/critic rears its ugly head. It cannot respond verbally to the left-brain. You must train your left-brain to give the right-brain what it needs to do its work: gentle questions related to the specifics of drawing and painting.

Remember a good painting will have lights, middles and darks.

You must establish the key or value range of your painting, preferably sooner than later.

Only when you're sure of a feature's proper placement should you go into more detail. Suggest the detail. Don't paint it.

When in the shadow side to get more form, go darker. When in the light, go lighter.

The beauty of reflections is in their subtlety. Avoid reflections jumping out at you by keeping them no lighter than your lightest shadow. They should never become more important than the major light and shadow patterns. The trick is to go darker around the reflection rather than lighter in the reflection itself.

Being specific and being detailed is not necessarily the same thing.

Remember, the sitter is always right. Pay attention. Look incessantly. Analyze.

Edges are the musical dance of a painting. Play with them. The edge quality must be considered wherever there is the slightest change of color. Edges happen between all forms and wherever there is a transition. They are the signatures of the painter. Go beyond "lost and found" edges. Experiment. Try a soft edge where you see a hard one, and vice-versa. Scrape it off. Try another edge. Don't be satisfied with the first thing that comes off your brush and don't be too predictable. On the other hand, learn to recognize an expressive edge when it happens.

Don't outline the edges of the mouth or the eyes. Look for openings where the edges are lost or fused into the surrounding areas of these features. They should never seem to be painted onto the face.

Follow your heart when it comes to hue. Follow your mind when it comes to value.

Emotion comes out in a painting without any prompting by the artist. I defy you to paint love, for instance. You can paint with love and hopefully that love will be expressed in the work.

In a portrait it is best to avoid unnecessary modeling in the background. Save that for the main event. Don't muddy up your halftones (the areas between light and shadow) with arbitrary blending. The best way to activate your halftones is with the addition of a definite color.

One definition of clutter: seemingly important details, which make the artist feel smart. Showing off can often lead to trouble.

It doesn't matter who comes up with the idea. It's who paints it.

Poetry without technique can leave us flat. Technique without poetry can leave us even flatter.

Let's not get lost in concepts or ideas, instead lose yourself in your senses, your perceptions, darks and lights, soft and hard edges, points related on a line, the way forms move through one another.

Neutrals set the stage for all the other hues. They set off the Reds and yellows of your palette.

The stroke of paint either describes a form or expresses an emotion. Ideally, it should do both.

Don't lose yourself in your art. Find yourself.

POINT OF ART

We don't want to ruin the magic trick of values. We don't want to see the strings holding up the magicians' floating object.

Look for dynamic edges. The edges help direct the eye where you want it to go.

Muddy, chalky paintings come about when we scrape into wet areas with too little paint on our brush. We end up mixing together the previous layers of paint.

In vegetation, look for reds (olive) or purples rather than blue. Blue should be avoided except in faraway objects on the horizon.

There's a time and place for "blending," but it should be done sparingly.

At no time in the process should you feel anything is set in concrete.

Remember, it's all about choices. The goal is to make a statement of yourself with every stroke. So be bold! Our goal is to say as much as we can with as few strokes as possible. Mushing paint together as you go along is a form of apology. You have nothing to apologize about; it's just a painting remember. Later, you will make an artistic decision where you want to soften certain edges. After you have layed in the mosaic of planes and forms you may feel the need to "humanize" or fuse certain edges here and there.

There are a number of ways to fuse or soften an edge, some more effective than others. Pulling darks into lights and vice versa is the most effective and most difficult way to fuse edges. Another method is to drag a rich half tone between the light and shadow planes. Another is to fuse edges with a clean brush, picking up the light on one side and the dark value on the other. The last, and least desirable way to fuse an edge, is to smudge it with a finger (even though this can sometimes be the most satisfying).

Jargon is so important. To tint a color means to add white. To tone is to add a neutral gray. Shading refers to the addition of black to a color.

When you add white (tint) it kills the chroma (which sometimes is better off dead). Add lighter valued, high chroma colors to your mixture to maintain full saturation, i.e. adding Cadmium Yellow to lighten Yellow Ochre. Consider the homeopathy of white. Try mixing white with a tint of blue, another white with a tint of green, then red, yellow, etc. Juxtapose these homeopathic colors, one next to the other, allowing your whites to vibrate. In this way, white is an opportunity to express a rainbow of subtle hues.

How does one achieve depth and focus in a painting? Use the forces of the feminine (yin) and the masculine (yang) to lead the eye where you want it to go:

- Vertical lines come forward. Horizontal lines recede.

- High chroma comes forward. Neutrality recedes.

- High contrast comes forward. Low contrast recedes.

- Hard edges come forward. Soft edges recede.

- Opaque paint comes forward. Thin paint recedes.

POINT OF ART

• Hard angles come forward. Rounded forms recede.

• Warm colors come forward. Cool colors recede.

Try not to let the texture become more important than the form.

Neutrals set the stage for all the other hues. They set off the Reds and yellows of your palette.

Don't color. Paint! Put the paint from your palette onto the painting. Deposit the paint. Trawl it in. Make a statement. Say, "This is who I am," with every stroke.

Only God can create beauty. At best the artist might hope to recognize and express it.

One way to achieving good color harmony is by making sure there is a little bit of each color throughout the painting. Cross pollinate colors in your paintings.

Please, your talent is worth far more than any amount of paint you may "waste."

Black, out of the tube, is a non-choice. It is better to mix combinations of Burnt Umber, Alizarim Crimson and Prussion Blue. Better yet, place these colors in juxtaposition with one another to create vibration of color in your dark accents.

On the other hand, using neutrals effectively is a skill it would behoove you to master.

Failure is the only road to success.

Look for warm accents in all organic forms.

The shape is where you hang your hat.

Cool light, warm shadow. Warm light, cool shadow.

Don't obsess, express!

The artist's job is to select from what already is, through the lens of his/her soul.

Skill is an illusion that takes years to buy into. And then, after all is said and done, it can rear its ugly head as an obstacle to full self-expression. The artist must learn to walk the line, precariously, between skill and fully abandoned self-expression.

Learning tip: look for the truth in what I say not in what I don't say. "Smart" people are sometimes the worst students.

First order of business: create an envelope, the outer parameter of the shape, into which the shape must be inserted.

The envelope is the essence, built on the gesture of the form. It consists of a series of straight lines at specific angles. The lines intersect where the shape turns, intersecting certain "sticky" points. The envelope is the structure of the head or the figure or the tree.

Value can express mood or form. Ideally, it must be used to express both.

Power Palette tip: Combine "flesh" color with red of the same value. Don't mix them on the palette. Rather, combine the like-valued hues on the painting itself. Don't beat them to death; let the complementary, like-valued hues vibrate together on the painting.

Don't be monogamous with color. Play the field. Live it up. Be a color whore.

POINT OF ART

Squint your eyes—see the form. Don't be seduced by texture, which is superficial. Form is synonymous with structure. Texture is the superficial element in painting.

The creative process is like riding a horse. You want the horse to go where you want but you don't want a dull ride.

It takes two artists to create a painting. One to do the painting and the other one to tell him when to stop. The art is being able to recognize the masterstroke.

Power Palette tip: muddiness occurs when you combine colors horizontally (value) across your palette, rather than vertically (like-valued hues).

All the answers to your questions about drawing can be found at the source—the model. The answer is not in your drawing/painting.

It's just as absurd to paint an "eye" as it is to paint a person's soul.

You can't paint a "thing" you can only observe and understand the abstract shapes and edges that make up the "thing."

Good drawing is the window to the soul.

The best realists are the best abstractionists. We must learn to distill forms down to their essence.

When it comes to drawing, its location, location, location.

The discipline of choice: make a choice so you can see if it fits. Take a stab. You can always choose to change. Remember, painting and drawing is not for sissies!

Straight lines are a choice; curved lines a decision. In a decision we select the lesser of two evils. With a choice there is only one option. Artists must learn to recognize the power of a choice versus the reasonableness of a decision.

Shut up and listen with your eyes! Listen to the right side of your brain. It knows. It doesn't have to decide or analyze. It sees shapes abstractly; it doesn't have to name them or categorize them. In fact, the right-brain sees abstract shapes instantaneously if you can get your left-brain critic out of the way and let it to its job.

Get hip to the zen of seeing.

Vague notions make for vague paintings. An idea is of no use unless it is crystal clear. Sometimes the process of painting leads us to these crystallizations; sometimes it leads us away. Work with your idea. Be open to it. Be gentle with it until it is ready. Then go after it like there's no tomorrow.

Squint your eyes to see the shapes, as if you were cutting them out with a pair of scissors. Squint your eyes as if you were squeezing forms into patterns of light and shadow. Design the shapes with absolute precision.

Think of the brain as your creative bank account. Food for the soul, such as theater, literature, concerts, etc., are deposits. Mindless activities like TV or other passive activities are withdrawals. Another creative withdrawal is attempting to render naturalistic images from the imagination. Without direct input from nature one is forced to invent and at worst fake the image into being. Nature herself is full of inspiration. A landscape, a human head, a still life are full of creative material which act as deposits into your creative bank account. Working from photo-graphs to the extent that it compromises the depth of visual and sensorial inputs, is also a creative withdrawal. The artist always must find his or her way back to nature in order to keep the work fresh and deep. We must constantly work to maintain a positive balance in our creative bank accounts.

In the under painting we are affecting values and color. We're not necessarily painting, in the purist sense of the word. The under painting, on the other hand, is an opportunity to paint like a watercolorist.

The spirit of the person is in the play of light. Get the value relationships and you're halfway to the essence of your subject.

The artist expresses himself in his edges. They convey the feeling of air and the texture.

Light conveys the form itself.

If you squint your eyes at it and you don't see it, it ain't there!

Paint with your eyes not your hands.

Let the shape burn itself into your retina. Then project it onto your painting like a laser beam.

The large shadow patterns are more important than the features because they express the bone and muscle structure of the subject. Without that structure there can be no form, no character, and no likeness.

The process of creating a work of art is the systematic satisfying of one need after another—which is why it's so gratifying. The self-talk goes like this: "I need to move this shape over here," or "I need to make this slightly darker than that," etc. Self-talk should not be, "I can't..." or "I should..." or "I wish I could..." etc.

Watch out for the tap dance beginners do on their paintings. The mechanical repetitious tapping of strokes, all in the same direction with the same energy and the same quality of edges, is the mark of mechanical and amateurish painting. Vary strokes, vary edges, vary the direction, size and distance between strokes.

When blending with the finger or fan brush or other tool you are manipulating edges. You are either adding variety or you are obliterating unnecessary forms. You must never blend as an apology for expression.

I love the different ways light interacts with substances like skin, hair, wood, air, liquids, metal and fabrics like silk, cotton, wool, denim, etc.

A series of well-executed naked strokes can create the illusion of 1,000 details.

Choices result from needs. Needs arise out of the process of exploration, which comes from a place of openness and freedom, which comes from setting goals and establishing a structure.

Drawing isn't about making a good copy of your subject as much as expressing a series of relationships. Drawing is a celebration of how things are connected.

POINT OF ART

Let us, the viewers, see the process of the drawing in the work.

Expressing the gesture of the form rather than copying its contours leads to emulation rather than mere mimicry.

Find the forms. They lead to character, which leads to likeness, which forms the foundation for expression of mood and personality.

It is either the right value or it isn't. Go with it. If it doesn't work change it. The worst thing is to "mush" it all together.

Mixing on the painting is great as an effect. The accidental brilliance of the unknown is very exciting. But in the hands of an inexperienced artist it can make for a chalky, muddy mess.

If you combine colors of the same value and chroma but different hues you'll create vibration and color harmony.

Artists are not detectives, who examine carefully every detail. As artists we have to see in broader strokes. An artist must learn to take pride in what he doesn't see.

Paint like a millionaire! Don't skimp when it comes to mixing your palette. Your experience and time is worth far more than the cost of paint.

"Visine" came along and said, "get the red out" and now we are stuck with it. In a commission portrait avoid too much red in and around the eyes.

Perfection is dull. There is no right or wrong in a work of art— no moral imperative. The artist is someone who can recognize when a "mistake" adds to the painting. The moralist can never be an artist.

One definition of quality: "adherence to a standard set of specifications." The artist must avoid perfection. Going after perfection may be admirable but sometimes it's better to take what you get along the way. This is the ultimate acknowledgment of a higher power. God lives in our imperfections.

Good defect is good effect.

Don't "finish" a passage. Resolve it.

Rule of composition—cut the figure the opposite way in which you would a chicken: never at the joint.

Where straight lines intersect is where your drawing occurs.

Keep your palette organized. The whole painting happens on the palette!

As an artist you are under no obligation to explain or justify what you are painting. You are here to paint, to express in paint who you are. Describe if you must but let's not insult the viewer with too much unnecessary detail or explanation.

Preciousness has no place in the process of painting. Painting is for warriors, not for the faint of heart.

An artist must learn how to use his tools like a surgeon, with the powerful combination of precision and urgency.

There are no concave shapes, only convex shapes. Look for convex shapes in all organic forms. All living things grow outward, even from the smallest cell to the most complex human forms. If it seems concave, look again. It is undoubtedly a combination of several convex shapes in convergence.

Design forms, playing negative space against positive (convex) shapes.

Don't be heavy handed when it comes to drawing. Tension kills expression.

It's all about honest observation. Look more at you subject while drawing. Looking at your drawing as you draw leads to the most self-conscious artifice. Practice blind contour drawing.

Work as if you are drawing the subject in mid-air rather than on paper.

Stick to shapes. Enjoy the particulars of your subject—honor the form. If you paint the form first the painting will progress much faster. Get off the texture—go for the form. Suggest the texture.

Go in like a commando, execute your stroke and get out.

If the value is just right you won't have to smoosh or blend the strokes together. Rather than blend, go back to the palette and apply just the right value halfway between each stroke in question.

Avoid compensating for incorrect values by mixing darker and lighter colors together on the painting. Rather, mix the correct value on your palette and deposit it over the incorrect value.

Remember, like-valued hues don't change form. They just vibrate in the eye.

Juxtapose colors rather than mix them. Let the viewer do the mixing.

Get the difference between perception and conception. Concept is a product of the left-brain. It is rooted in language and the literary. Visual perception is the function of the right-brain. Both sides are necessary. Both are creative but each side performs a completely different function.

Glaze a rainbow. Prepare your glazes by applying a medium of equal parts linseed oil, turpentine and retouch varnish. Allow for subtle gradations of transparent colors. Don't mix them to death before applying.

The most important moment in the painting is the start. Practice starting. Work with thumbnails or better yet, draw the figure from life—quick poses, two-to five minutes each.

If you don't fall in love with your subject, the painting will always be somehow arduous.

What attracts us to our subject is its peculiar eccentric way of being. That is what we are painting.

Avoid the glib summary: "the grass is green," "the sky is blue" etc. These labels reside in the left-brain and are a throwback to our childhood. Unless you intend to remain a primitive, or outsider artist, then we need to retrain your way of seeing to include the million-hued variations that exist in nature and in our imaginations.

Let the paint itself make the texture. Get out to the way of the paint.

If you can identify what you don't know—then guess what? You know it!

Let the shapes tell the story.

POINT OF ART

Listen with your eyes. Always go back to the source. When you squint you see only the principal shapes. You see what's important.

The key to releasing the imagination is in embracing structure.

Look at things in their context. Otherwise we may wander off on tangents.

People who say they "know what they like" are really saying they "like what they know."

There is "what we know we know," "what we know we don't know" and "what we don't know we don't know." We are the experts only of our own realm. Our intuition is only good for revealing what we already know. It's not what you don't know that stops you. It's what you don't know you don't know that stops you. To get to a higher intuitive level we need to constantly be increasing our knowledge base.

The artist is a person who is committed to structure and stays on purpose. On the other hand he/she is capable of recognizing what might be called "happy accidents." This detachment from the result is a direct communion with our higher power.

Do your thinking on your palette. Don't think so much on your painting. Painting is doing.

Study the psychology of composition. We direct the eye, leading the viewer on an optical journey through the painting. We must create an entry point and a route the eye can take through the painting. The object is to keep the viewer engaged on many levels. In order to do so we must give thought to their journey. This then becomes our journey.

We want to draw the viewer in and keep him/her engaged long enough to "get" what you want him/her to get.

It's not about pleasing the viewer. It's about getting and keeping him/her engaged and invested in the artwork. In this sense, every passage is a piece of marketing.

In the beginning, go for the structure. Save the affect for later.

Value-based painting frees us up. If we focus our conscious mind on value, it takes the pressure off worrying about hue and chroma. Hence, we are then free to be truly creative with color!

When it comes to hue, look for the exception not the stereotype. Grass is rarely green and the sky is rarely blue.

Drawing and painting have nothing to do with media. One can paint with a pencil and draw with a brush. Drawing is a matter of relating lines and shapes while painting is concerned with relating values and edges.

To control form you must learn to control value.

Without the proper setup the master stroke is meaningless.

When painting a brick wall we first paint the mass color of brick. Then we suggest a few bricks. This idea has many applications for numerous subjects.

POINT OF ART

For example, don't paint hair. Design it. Look for the larger forms. Once you have those in place you can suggest a hair or two.

Don't overuse pure neutral gray as a hue, in and of itself.

Neutrals are primarily used to set off the surrounding hues, i.e. to make the reds seem redder, etc. Remember, everything is relative.

The power of positive painting means to paint with purpose and intention.

Combining complements will create either mud or color vibration, depending on how you use them. Hint: like-valued complementary hues tend to vibrate.

Choose a structure. Work with your choices. Looseness should never be confused with sloppiness.

Consider the anatomy of a landscape. It's not arbitrary. Relate forms together the way you would in figurative work, with the same amount of commitment.

Ultimately, the painting lives or dies in its design.

Think of your format as a box—now paint outside the box. We need to suggest the world outside the world of the painting. Our painting is merely a glimpse of the real world. Translation: allow the shapes that live in your painting to go over the edges of the format.

Paint quality: think of your brush as a trawl, and you are a bricklayer. Deposit the paint onto the painting. Leave something of yourself behind on the surface of the paint itself.

Use your sables like a trawl. Lay the paint like a bricklayer builds a wall.

Not so "honk your horn" green!

The way to be a conscious painter (not self-conscious) is to compose in a thumbnail, prepare a palette, create a structure. Be intentional. Then, allow things to happen. Meanwhile, if you're going to break a rule or throw out a structure, have a good reason.

We must consider the background as part of the composition.

The negative spaces are what make or break the design. And the design is everything. The background must not be an afterthought. It is there to create a context that leads our eye to the main event.

A lot of portraits have been painted where the value of the face in shadow is the same as the value in the background. While this is not always the case, it's something to consider.

In the rendering we can't lose sight of the materials. I need to feel I can trust that I'm in the hands of a master of the materials.

We're creating an architectural structure in a specific universe.

Don't let your choices of hard/soft edges be too arbitrary.

Edges are used to lead the eye of the viewer. You cannot relinquish this responsibility.

What good is full saturation of color, without a strong sense of value/form.

POINT OF ART

Pastel can sometimes become very "pastel." Don't blend so much.

It's easy to find yourself painting "things" rather than shapes. This is the mark of an amateur.

How does one paint "happiness?" Let's not be too literal. There's nothing more dangerous than an overzealous attempt to paint literal feelings.

Over articulated, individual shapes can confuse the eye and ruin the sense of oneness.

Sometimes it can be too picture-postcard-perfect to be effective as "art."

It's difficult to paint a sunset. The least you can do is to make sure the horizon is straight.

The impossibility of the horizon curving downward takes me out of the universe you intended to create.

Nice exuberant paint quality. Falls a little flat in the design department.

The weight of the picture needs to match the size. The larger size of the rendering requires more thought and planning.

The rendering of the swan is lovely. Placement is just so-so.

This is an ordinary rendering of an extraordinary scene. I'd rather it be the other way around.

You're just shy of succeeding in what you seem to be intending.

Too wide a variety of styles take me out of the universe of the picture.

Is this a work of extraordinary significance? What aren't you saying about the time of day, subject or place that needs to be said?

That's a lovely rendering of flowers but we've seen it before.

Confusion around edges inhibits the eye's ability to navigate through the work. Too many hard edges in the wrong places stop the eye cold.

Nice to look at but it's verging more on the decorative rather than the artistic.

Don't let the work become too "techniquey."

Very sellable but is it an extraordinary work of art?

Technically, lacks the sense of form and light, time of day. You establish these as goals for the work but do not realize them in the paint.

Where is the extraordinary reason for being?

The lack of color harmony leads to being too literal with colors.

Are the flowers in the same universe as the background?

POINT OF ART

Don't let the skill of execution fall behind the quality of the idea.

As a color field it is very seductive.

A lack of skill takes us out of the universe of the picture. Too much skill can do it just as easily.

Don't express just for expression's sake. Instead express a love of form or materials. Find a structure you can be passionate about.

Don't let the composition be too predictable.

Good drawings almost always possess a variety of line quality (thickness).

Let's not be too literal with color, i.e. orange tree, white birch.

What are you saying about a sunset that hasn't been said before? What are you saying about atmosphere, temperature, feeling of water?

An unimportant shape seems to have found its way to the dynamic focal point. Who's driving this car?

The frame is taking away. Available frames are not always the best frames.

Clarify your vision. In what universe does this scene exist?

Go for the un-self-conscious line. Don't monitor yourself so carefully. Let go. Feel the force within you.

That's a lovely rendering of flowers, but what would elevate this to the level of fine art?

Check color perspective. Things in the distance are too dark, too warm and too distinct.

You're being primitive, while not meaning to be. Strive to be more specific in developing responsive drawing skills. Look for structure lines in your drawings. Or, just relax and become the best primitive artist you can be.

Without extensive experience drawing from life your figures will never have a convincing sense of wholeness and relationships of forms one to another. Draw from life whenever you can.

How does one create an extraordinary experience with the materials of visual art?

Art is what happens along the way to mastering a structure.

The artist is someone who recognizes a good thing when it happens and has just enough skill to create the circumstances where expression can happen.

Each work of art requires its own kind of craft, depending on the intentions of the artist. If you are trying to convey a stormy day, you might do well to understand color perspective. If you want to pull us into the figure, better draw from life. Too much craft can be equally dangerous. Being an artist is to walk a thin line between chaos and structure. Mastery is knowing when to take control and when to give it up.

Structure creates the opportunity for freedom.

Some Advice on Selling Art

Making money doing what you love—what's wrong with this?

If art is therapy then the sale is the catharsis.

Selling, giving or throwing away your art is the completion of the creative cycle.

Art is the excrement of the creative process.

The goal of art is to communicate—to move, touch and inspire. Inspiration has a value.

Consider profit as the measure of your contribution to humanity.

Buying art is not as much about filling an empty space on your wall as it is about filling an empty space in your soul.

Every work of art has a story to tell. Allow the buyer to discover it.

One of the many problems with our society is that it places more importance on things that have a price than on things that have a value.

An entrepreneur is speculative; there is no attachment to the products he/she creates. A business owner creates a business in order to do what he/she loves. The business owner serves the art, yet the business is separate from his/her art. The professional artist is both an entrepreneur and a business owner.

Don't sell. Don't persuade. Be of service to the collector.

Selling is a question and answer process—listening, mirroring and clarifying.

All statements you make should end with a tie-down question: "this is an excellent example of expressionism, don't you think?"

Don't quibble over interpretation. Educate, yes, but remember, the buyer is always right.

Never assume someone isn't a buyer.

Determine the global values—what motivates your buyer? i.e. love, esteem, status, beauty, inspiration, exclusivity, individuality/identity, pride/respect. What are his/her primary concerns or what is he/she afraid of? i.e. fitting in, keeping under budget, making the right choice, matching the décor.

Use visualization: "Where do you think you might hang the piece?" "Can't you just see the looks on their faces when they see this on your wall?" "This will make a powerful statement about your company, don't you think?"

You must create an urgent opportunity for the collector.

What are the components of an effective goal? Ask the following questions. Why is this goal important or meaningful? How is it measurable? Is it achievable? Is it fluid (is there an opportunity to modify it if circumstances change)? Does it have a deadline or timeframe? How will you accomplish it (this is your action plan)? How will you celebrate when it's accomplished?

Example of an effective goal: "I will paint 5 large narrative paintings in 3 months and celebrate by taking my wife out to a very nice restaurant." "I will close (see below for what a close is) 10 prospects per month for one year and at the end of that year I will buy myself an I-phone."

You must learn to close a sale. A close is an invitation to action within a certain timeframe. Here are some example closes:

"Would you like to go ahead with it today?" "Would you like to put a deposit on it tonight?" "Are you ready to place a red dot now?" If you don't close, you are very unlikely to uncover the buyer's objections. If you don't know what his/her objections are you are unlikely to sell your artwork.

This is one common objection: "it's too much money." Here's a possible response: "I know how how you FEEL. I have FELT the same way. It's not easy having expensive tastes. What I've FOUND is most of my clients, after everything is said and done, are glad they invested their money into a meaningful art collection."

The value must be equal to cost for the sale to be possible.

Determine if in fact, cost is the only concern with the following question: "What else is standing in the way of your getting what you want tonight?" Or, "how far apart are we on the value of this artwork?" Determine that difference in dollars.

Generate good word-of-mouth by including a surprise along with the purchase. Give them an extra print, a small painting, or a certificate of provenance. People are often more inclined to talk about their experience with you if you surprise them with a little more than they bargained for.

Never offer discounts for nothing. Trade a discount for something of equal value to you—barter. Offer a discount for going ahead right now. You may discount for waiting on delivery while you exhibit the work. You can also discount if they agree to host a vernissage (a party where the artwork is unveiled in front of his/her friends at which you are present).

Part 2: Essays

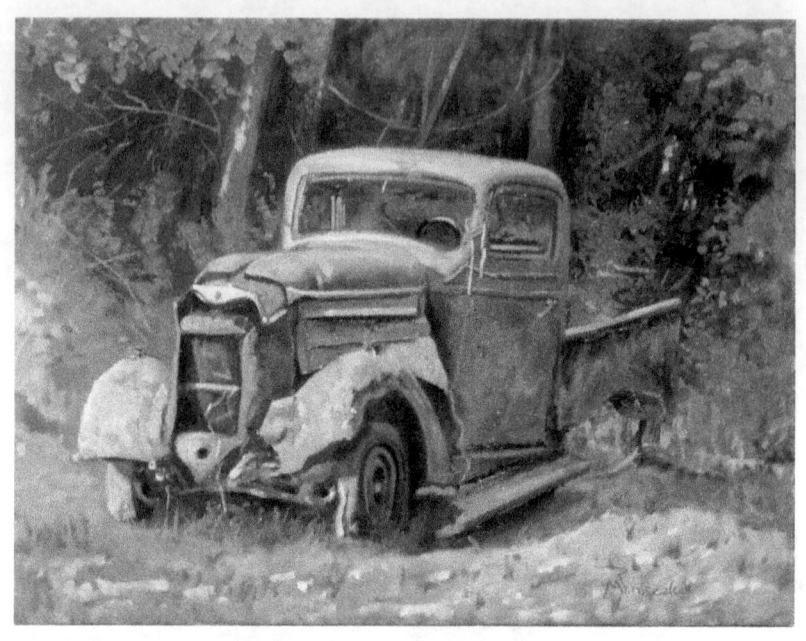

37 Chevy 16" x 20"

Always Be in Action

Being in action is the key to getting the "art" monkey off your back. Don't forget, you got into painting because it gave you pleasure. Let's get back to thinking of art as a process that gives us pleasure by addressing specific goals, one at a time. We cannot make art in order to impress the juror at the local art guild or in order to look good in front of our friends. In other words, we must leave our ego at the door. We must distract our ego by getting into action and staying there.

By the way, it may also help you to know that you are already a member of the club, the artistic elite. You may as well accept that you are whole and complete already; there's no one to impress; no pre-requisites, or magic passwords or "dues to pay" to become an artist. The moment you choose to be an artist is when you become an artist. Being an artist isn't a destination; it is a state of being. Kurt Vonnegut once wrote, "we are what we pretend to be." In many ways, it's a confidence game.

If you want to win the "art" game you must have the vision to accept that you've already won it. If you can imagine that you already are a great painter, that you are simply recalling the process of becoming one, it will make things a whole lot easier. Have you ever had the feeling that you already knew a piece of information presented by a teacher you respect? New information should be greeted with the feeling that you are being reminded of something you already knew on some level. That's where the access to your talent lies. It's a safe place, off limits from your ego. There's no conflict with your ego because everything already is as it should be. All that's left is the joy of learning and doing.

This detachment is essential if we are going to approach a blank canvas as each technical and creative problem presents itself. I'm talking about the Zen law of detachment, which says that only when we are ready to release our grip on our desired outcome (i.e. "great art") will we be ready to learn the skills and insights needed to achieve it.

What we don't need is pressure to create "great" art. The fact is it doesn't matter whether it's good or bad, at least not while you are in the middle of the process. Reserve judgment of the whole while you're working on the parts. Remember, it's just canvas, paints, brushes and a little time spent doing what you love. When you're all done with your painting you can put on your critic's hat and tear it to pieces. Better yet, recognize that a good critic doesn't judge. His/her job is to describe what's wrong, specifically and compassionately, with the painting. The ego should have no place in this process.

Originality:
Copying vs. Interpreting

One of the most debilitating issues we face is the question of originality. "Has this been done before?" Did you know that a restaurant is allowed to serve canned soup and call it "home-made?" All they have to do is add one ingredient. The same is true for artists. According to copyright law if you change one element in an image, painted or photographic, it becomes your image. This should take a bit of the weight of originality off your shoulders. It's much more difficult not to be original; I've never seen two paintings of flowers that were exactly alike, except perhaps at a starving artist sale! Try copying a masterpiece. It's actually easier to paint it in a new way. One might conclude, in this context, that our lack of skill is an asset.

While it's true that human beings are not really capable of truly "copying" anything it is also true there is really nothing new under the sun. The moment an image enters your eye and goes into your brain it has undergone a transformation called interpretation. When it comes out through your hand it undergoes another transformation called execution. Interpretation and execution are the extra ingredients that make something original. So when you're faced with a blank canvas don't sabotage yourself into thinking you have to come up with something brand new to be considered original.

What is your style, your vision? Style has everything to do with your particular choices. What will you include and what will you exclude from your realm of vision? What is most essential to the painting? Are you painting what's important to you? This is your style.

Go to the local library or museum, open a book, take a look around you. Pay attention. Be open. Look for opportunities. They're all around you. As the saying goes, "it's not what you paint, it's how you paint it." Have you ever heard someone look at a Picasso and say, "hell, I could have done that." Whenever I hear that my response is always the same: "but you didn't do it, Picasso did." Sometimes it's not even necessarily what you paint or how you paint it that distinguishes your work as original, it's that you painted it at all!

The other side of the coin is about eccentricity: the ability to look at the same thing everyone else sees and shift the angle, the point of view, just enough to make it yours. It is always a worthwhile exercise to ask yourself what you could do with your setup/subject to give it a little spin.

The common theme up to now can be summed up in one word: tenacity. It takes a lot of nerve to make art. Whether you're doing abstract expressionism or photo-realism you will be more successful if you are tenacious. Skill and creativity are the result of hard work and dedication. Tenacity is the incomprehensible belief that you already have what it takes, the blind courage to take bold action and the absolute willingness to fail, spectacularly.

POINT OF ART

As for talent, it is nothing more than a strong inner voice that grants us permission to do exactly what we feel like doing in our art. It is guided by a strong desire to communicate. It is a commitment to the authentic self; a willingness and openness to look more deeply, to be present to ourselves and the world around us. It is a supreme sensitivity to our inner most thoughts and feelings. It is a trust that our inner creative spirit will guide us to the truth and it's a promise that "the truth will set us free." Talent is having the courage to assert what is true for you, right now. The secret to creativity is to accept that we really don't actually have access to absolute truth. There's no point in pretending that we do. This humility frees us up for real creativity because it acknowledges that we are only one part of something larger than ourselves. Few individuals are willing to do this. Nonetheless, it is available to all of us if we are willing to accept our truth as we see it at this moment.

Tenacity and talent can be developed if we are willing to let go of our attachment to the result. Stanislavski, the great teacher of "method acting," once said, "find the art in yourself not yourself in the art." In other words, stay focused on what you are doing, not that you are doing (or failing to do) it.

With representational, for example, the ego rears its ugly head when we find ourselves taking pride in our ability to paint "things." The ego takes pride in painting a nose. This is the big pitfall. The artist never paints a nose. We are painting shapes, colors, forms, edges that, taken as a whole, create the illusion of a nose.

Managing the ego is essential for artistic freedom; this freedom is a precious gift that's yours the moment you let go of the pressure to create a "great" work of art. Therefore, fellow artists, accept that ours is but to do.

The Easy Way
vs. The Right Way

My father once said, "there's the right way to do something and there's the easy way." I found this confusing when I was young because this statement can be interpreted a number of ways. At first glance "easy" and "right" are placed at odds with one another. But are they? "Easy" and "right" are not necessarily mutually exclusive. The fact of the mater is the "right" way is almost always the "easy" way. I think my father said this to me in the hope that I would not take short cuts along the way, that I might learn to appreciate hard work.

I have found that those who achieve greatness have learned the secret of how to work economically and effectively. Talent, then, might be defined as the ability to identify a problem, break it down into manageable components and enter the process of resolving each problem, one at a time. In short, great artists have

the ability to develop an effective working method. What my father was really trying to tell me is that we must learn to work "easy" and "right." It is the difference between wanting something and wanting to want something. Be honest. Ask yourself, on some level, "do I enjoy struggling as an artist?" The answer may surprise you. Many of us believe we have to struggle with something for it to be worthwhile, when all we really need is the necessary information presented in a way we can understand and assimilate. This is the key to finding the right way and the easy way.

The Power of Positive Painting

The *Power of Positive Painting* method is a distillation of the concepts and ideas of Frank J. Reilly (1906-1967), whose emphasis on the effective use of values to create the illusion of form, laid the foundation for many of today's most successful representational artists and illustrators. Although he never wrote it down, many of Reilly's disciples have written books on his method and theories. Reilly was part of the lineage of illustrator/ artists like Howard Pyle and NC Wyeth. The system was passed down to me through my father, internationally known portrait artist, Joseph Maniscalco. The Reilly method was an attempt to develop a common language for artists, a set of standards by which representational artists could establish a solid foundation of seeing and expressing the natural world.

In order to use color effectively we must understand its various components. All colors have a specific hue, value and chroma. Albert H. Munsell, (1858-1918) devised a system of measuring and identifying these various components of color to take the guesswork out of matching or describing a color. The Munsell system became the standard used by the Bureau of Weights and Measures for printing in the early 1900s.

Value-based painting means we are emphasizing the lightness or darkness of color over the other elements. In other words, we are not distracting ourselves with vague, poetic descriptions of color like "beige", "scarlet", "puce," or even terms like "bright orange," which are very subjective. In fact, any color can be assigned a number sequence representing its hue, value and chroma. The 12 basic hues are described simply, for example, R for red, RO for reddish orange, etc. All colors from the color wheel can be expressed by a value range from 0 to 10. There is also a scale of 0 to 18 that expresses a color's chroma, the degree it departs from neutral gray. All colors can be described with the hue, along with its numeric value/chroma. Cadmium Red out of the tube, for instance is "R 5/14," (depending upon the brand).

Cad. Red or R 5/14 is the most intense chroma possible with Red. Keep in mind it is a relatively dark color, a value of 5, right in the middle of our scale. To use red in lighter passages you have to add white, which reduces its chroma.

The Power Palette is a reduction of neutrals, reds, yellows and "flesh" colors arranged by value. Keep in mind, any and all colors, in all temperatures, from our color wheel can be expressed in 10 corresponding values. You can use the Munsell system to identify and mix the exact color you are trying to match in your subject., ask yourself, "do I need to add more blue, red or yellow? Is it higher or lower in chroma?" and most importantly, "is it lighter or darker?" By far, the most difficult to see and most illusive aspect of color is its value. But it can be learned, like a musician learns his scales. Musicians train the ear to hear, we must train our eye to see.

Note: you can find color charts and more information on this value-based painting system on my website:
www.maniscalcogallery.com

When Is a Painter an Artist?

I finally read "Zen and the Art of Motorcycle Maintenance." I may not be performing a tune-up anytime soon, but it has really impressed me in terms of what I do, namely paint in the "classical" tradition. Author, Robert M. Pirsig distinguishes "Romantic" beauty, as the appearance that strikes the senses, from "Classic" beauty, which comes out of a harmonious order of the parts.

Representational artists, like me, have often been made to feel "square" because we aren't "cool" and spontaneous; we can't throw paint around like a guerilla (or a gorilla). We are not "romantic," by the definition above. The book has taught me to value my having a rational, classical method and offers a reconciliation of these two approaches. Obviously there needs to be a balance. I'm not here to invalidate the sincere efforts of any of my splatter-painting colleagues. What needs to be present in any artistic endeavor, however, is an authenticity, the presence of something called quality.

Pirsig asserts that quality is actually what generates our perception of reality. It is not merely a response to "reality," a judgment, as we were taught to believe in school. It is a pre-intellectual awareness. Ever wonder why the first thing that pops into our head when we look at a work of art is either "I like it" or "I don't?" It is an emotional response. Before there is understanding there is an awareness of and attraction to quality.

John Singer Sargent's monk-like devotion to achieving a perfect, spontaneous eloquence in every stroke is an example that comes to mind. As a portrait artist, I can appreciate the effort, the working and reworking that went into creating the appearance of effortlessness in his best work. It would never occur to most viewing a Sargent how much underlying structure and "science" went into making his paintings. There was an immense commitment to finding the balance between romantic and classical beauty. These diametrically opposed approaches are clearly reconciled in the work of creative genius like Sargent. Sure it can be said that quality is "whatever you like." But it's also true that what a genius "likes" contains a world of experience that informs his every scribble.

Juxtaposed in my reading room is another great book for painters, published by Stove Prairie Press, called "Alla Prima, Everything I know About Painting" by Richard Schmid. He too is a masterful painter. Two questions arise as I read these books in tandem: is it possible to be a good painter and not be a good artist? And the other: is it possible to be a great artist and not be a good painter? Schmid has nothing profound to say about his subjects. It's just delicious to look at. It is his sensitivity and expressiveness in paint that makes his work profound. He masterfully observes what is important and essential and gets it down on canvas with an elegant authority. Ostensibly, he operates in the world of appearances, which according to Pirsig makes him a "Romantic." But he executes his paintings with the depth of understanding and skill that can only be termed "Classical." Schmid makes this Romantic/Classical reconciliation look easy.

But is he an artist? Absolutely. It's the romantic/classical reconciliation that makes him so.

I know many who would say no, he's just a glorified copyist. While this may be said of many realists working today, it can't be said of Richard Schmid. I'm getting pretty bored with those artists who bang away at splatter painting and random stabs of color, turning down their noses at anyone who's taken the time to get under the hood, as it were, and learn the craft of painting. Yes, on one hand, art is "whatever you want it to be." But it needs to be so much more. Otherwise, why all the fuss? Schmid asserts that "'looseness' should be the way a painting appears, not how it is accomplished."

It's funny how the critics of representational artists accuse them of having nothing deep or profound to say—what does a beautifully painted landscape really tell us about being human? On the other side of the abyss, representationalists accuse conceptual or abstract artists of a similar lack of depth. Where, for example, is the art in dragging a piece of wood behind a car and then hanging it on a wall? We're asked to accept that it's not the wood board but the experience it represents. But is it art? Sure, why not?

Ultimately, great art must create its own universe, one in which the artist has completely invested him/herself. This is where art lives or dies. The jolt of that immediate gratification of appearance combined with an understanding of the underlying structure and meaning makes for a Zen-like experience when it comes to creating and enjoying serious art. It's also great for riding and maintaining motorcycles.

Some Advice on Collecting Fine Art

Great original art gives and lives inside the owner. It distinguishes him/her as an individual. It's best to become informed by utilizing museums, galleries, auction houses, other collectors, art books & periodicals. What is the state of the current art scene? Allow yourself to form opinions. The bottom line must be what turns you on. Do you enjoy subjective or abstract art? Is there an historical period that appeals to you or are you interested in what is being done today (contemporary)? Will your collection focus on a particular region, medium or subject? Do you prefer a certain genre, i.e. impressionism, expressionism, realism. Many people prefer to build an eclectic collection, whereas others prefer to specialize in one type of art. Be careful to avoid fashion trends.

What do you need to look for in a work of art? There are many ways to appreciate and determine quality in fine art. Depending on the artwork in question some elements are more important than others. Breaking a work down into its elemental parts, however, is essential. What is the aesthetic and historical relevance? Aspects such as composition, color, surface, mannerliness, and expressiveness are very important in an abstract piece. Whereas, the narrative, subject, paint quality, play of light or draftsmanship might be more important in realism. Become acquainted with the jargon of art. Understand the difference and function of "decorative art" vs. "fine art." Be concerned about archival quality—will it stand up over time? Learn to recognize quality in all its aspects.

The value of a work of art is not necessarily the same as its cost. As with any purchase the art consumer is looking for the value to be greater than the cost. Or, put another way, equity is the difference between the purchase price and the appraisal value. Art collectors are savvier today, not as subject to hype and the empty promises of huge investment turn-arounds. Even though art collecting is still one of the best long term investments around it is unrealistic to buy art for the sole purpose of making a financial killing. The bottom line is this: is the personal satisfaction and value you will derive from owning the work of art worth the cost? Watch out for dubious Limited edition prints or starving artist fare, dressed up to look like art.

What makes for a good art investment? In contemporary circles, one determines prices based on the quality of art, the stature of the artist (gallery/museum shows, awards, notoriety, collections, provenance of works, etc) and the fair market value of his/her work. Emerging artists are a good long-term investment if their work is of consistently high quality and if the artist has proven he/she is on a solid career track.

An investment in art will likely appreciate if the work in question has beauty and originality in its favor. Did you know that five percent of the population controls 90 percent of the wealth; these people buy and sell art. Do they know something we don't know? Don't throw your money away but don't be part of the woulda, coulda, shoulda club either. Trust your instincts. How many great pleasures, how many opportunities have passed you by because you didn't trust your instincts? Great artists have a way of tapping into the pleasure centers of the brain. Collecting their art is a kick. If you've been sitting on the bench, get into the game!

Is Art Cool?

I'm not a cool person. They can dress me up to look cool. I've played cool on TV. But I'm really not cool. That's ok, I'm cool with it. On the other hand, with all this talk about "cool cities" I thought we should take a moment to deconstruct cool. Trouble is, even the word "deconstruct" is no longer cool, so this isn't going to be easy. But I'm cool with that, too.

The difficulty is that cool is like silence: the moment you speak its name it is no longer there. It is the ephemeral nature of cool that concerns me most, particularly since we have now firmly planted the future of arts funding in the soil of cool.

Advertisers drive themselves crazy trying to determine the latest in cool. Cool is a pretty tricky commodity. It's like the old adage: "I don't know anything about art but I know what I like." We know cool when we see it. Nevertheless, cool is subjective. Cool is temporary. Cool is indefinable by its very nature.
If we take a look at the word itself we can see the problem. To be cool is to be detached in an apathetic way. Cool people let things slide. They hang loose. Nothing bothers them. It's all cool. Cool people like to think of themselves as unique but they're not. By definition, cool people lack passion, which is really cool if you want to follow the crowd. But that's cool.

POINT OF ART

Cool people get along in life without too much hassle. They know how to keep their cool. When others are getting all up in your face about not-so-cool stuff like war, moral values and social security, cool people manage to stay pretty cool. While I think I'm pretty cool with people who are cool I'm also cool with those who aren't. Tolerance, it seems, is no longer cool, which is totally uncool.

Sometimes it seems nothing I do is cool. For instance, when I see a painting or listen to a musical composition that is clearly intended to be shocking I'm happy to report I'm still able to find it within myself to actually express shock. Being shocked is definitely not cool. Remember the now famous depiction of the Virgin Mary made with cow dung? That shocked a lot of people; they got on their high horse and made a big fuss. That wasn't too cool. Then Mayor Giuliani even tried to close down the museum.

Clearly, these people weren't being cool. Most never bothered to look at the work. We've got Liberals refusing to see that Mel Gibson Passion movie and the religious right refusing to watch the latest Michael Moore flick. Despite this lack of direct exposure, neither faction has a problem criticizing the other's efforts. It seems no one is really cool any more.

I wonder if it's even possible for human beings to get upset and still be cool about allowing others to express themselves. That would be cool. The ACLU isn't cool but I'm sure glad they're out there fighting for my freedom to not be cool if I want.

Frankly, I think being cool is overrated. That's why I'm just a little concerned about the "cool cities" bit, the movement to encourage cities to support grassroots arts and uplift the creative community. It feels like we're trying desperately to fit artists into just another neat, harmless little category, which has no real meaning. Is it possible we are eviscerating ourselves by suggesting the arts are cool or that the arts have some unique power to attract cool people? Aren't we further marginalizing our importance to society by embracing this dubious label? Sure, we'd all like to think we were cool. But the artists I know are anything but cool.

Artists are hot. They are bothered. Most have something to say and damn it they're going to say it. That's what it means to be an artist. I'm aware there's another dimension to the word cool, however. It's the thing great marketers are banking on; it's also what the cool cities people are hoping people recognize: there's a part of us that celebrates the mavericks, the visionaries—those bold few who have the tenacity to put art galleries in dilapidated old buildings—in long forgotten sections of a troubled city. I was even silly enough (or bold enough) to open a serious art gallery in Grosse Pointe, a place where few had ever succeeded. I thought, "Let's bring cool to Grosse Pointe." Well, after struggling to stay in business for eight years I'm not so sure how cool an idea that was. In reality, there's very little that's cool about setting yourself apart from the pack. I get a kick out of the way Gary Larsen expressed this notion as a befuddled cow, literally "out, standing in his field." Being cool can be pretty lonely at times.

There is something definitely inspiring about discovering and being part of a happening, stimulating arts scene. That's what the arts community has committed itself to—call it what you will. One thing is certain: art is eternal. Cool, on the other hand, may not always be cool. It is a word, full of sound and fury, signifying nothing.

The Next Generation of Artists

I am often asked for advice from parents who want to develop their child's full creative potential. True, it is now a widely accepted fact that the arts demand a child to use his/her whole brain, leading to a more well-rounded, tolerant adult. Children with little or no exposure to the formal study in disciplines such as the visual arts, writing, music or dance, are being cheated of their full potential.

Occasionally, parents of children interested in a more serious commitment, a burning desire to be a professional artist, approach me. What advice can I give them? My answer usually begins with advising them about building a foundation of basic fundamentals and ends with suggesting they find themselves a mentor.

I am a product of a successful apprenticeship with my father, Joseph Maniscalco. I was lucky to have a father who is a master painter as well as a patient teacher and generous colleague. Together our professional careers span a combined 80 years. Naturally, if they are so inclined, I look forward to working long side my children as they develop creatively. One of the most gratifying aspects of running an art gallery was the opportunity to mentor emerging artists as they evolved into mature professional artists.

Finding one's own voice as an artist is a journey toward authenticity with quite a few worthwhile stops along the way. So, my advice to someone starting out is to find a master whose work you respect. Be sure it's a good fit, then make them an offer they cannot refuse. Offer to do their dirty work, stretch their canvases, clean their studio, reorganize their files, balance their checkbook—whatever. Make yourself indispensable. If that doesn't work, money comes in handy. Some experienced professionals offer career coaching and critiquing as a fee-based service. We need to recognize that experienced artists are professionals and that their time and expertise is valuable.

Many experienced artists present intensive workshops or classes where students can get individual attention and nurturing. In exchange for these fees and/or services rendered you can study with them, observe their process, pick their brains, take the thing they do—that you admire—and make it your own. When it's time, move onto the next master who has a technique, an approach, something you'd like to incorporate into what you want to do.

Find a coach. One of the greatest coaches of all time, Vince Lombardi, once defined coaching as "getting someone to do what they don't want to do so they can do what they've always wanted to do."

Apprenticeships and mentorships can take many forms. There are often local organizations which work within their community, offering mentorship programs, pairing masters with promising students at little or no cost.

Mentorship opportunities are not always so easy to recognize. Sometimes we have to use our imaginations and be a little persistant in making them happen. A wonderful example of a unique mentorship is the story of Grosse Pointe artist Jac Purdon and my wife, Amanda Maniscalco. Jac is a master of conceptual art and

74

a longtime friend. A few years ago, when he lost his wife, Carol, Amanda and I naturally wanted to spend time with him and somehow help him—and us—get through the devastating loss of this extraordinary woman. Around this time Amanda was experimenting with the materials of her trade, custom framing.

She began carving mats into interesting forms and asked Jac or advice on what to do with them. A great, collaborative relationship was born and her conceptual work blossomed. She began peopling her forms with tiny figures and objects that told stories and evoked ideas. She even found there was a demand for what she was producing. The process also helped Jac in his healing process. Mentorships are a great example of how the creative process can be a powerful healing force.

Another great mentorship that started at College for Creative Studies, between celebrated abstract artist, Gilda Snowden and Jocelyn Rainey, developed into an example of the life-transforming power of art. Jocelyn's life had taken a tragic turn. She was the victim of an attempted murder. Through her adversity she discovered her inner vision with Gilda's loving guidance and is now considered among Detroit's top artists in her own right.

All great careers are built on the heels of masters who have come before. I suggest that young artists not be in a hurry to strike out on their own too quickly—because striking out is probably what they will do. I can't tell you how many times people have walked into my gallery, paintings tucked under each arm, staring straight at the floor, boasting of how they have never taken an art lesson in their lives and how "original" their work is as a result. Let me say in all fairness, there is a considerable niche for what is called "outsider art," art that comes from outside academia, otherwise known as primitive art. I have known and exhibited a number of outsider artists. In fact, there are a number of galleries and museums across the country that specialize in this particular genre. There are a number of outsider geniuses whose work is truly unique and extraordinary. But for the most part these are the rare exceptions.

Think about it like this: nobody would expect to be treated by an unqualified doctor. Nor would they want to have his or her car fixed by an unqualified mechanic. But when it comes to the artist there are a lot of unqualified people showing and selling their work. Their only qualification is that they have a passion to paint. This phenomenon occurs in other artistic disciplines as well, such as acting. In this way, the art business is a bit of a confidence game. There is little agreement as to what makes an artist qualified. We may or may not be correct in assuming someone who has gone through art school or received a university education has come out with a qualification in fine art. On the other hand, do you have to be qualified to laugh, cry, be surprised, whistle or sing? Identifying qualifications for artists is a slippery slope at best. Ultimately, an artist must be judged on the quality of the work itself.

Interestingly, I have found that the term "academic," which used to refer to those who studied the fundamentals of drawing from casts, then from life, who studied painting systems and design, who mastered the materials and pursued a course laid out by the great artists and teachers of classical realism, is now considered outside academia. Today, "academia" refers to those who have received an advanced degree from an accredited institution where they have learned how to throw caution to the wind and paint just like De Kooning or Pollock, trying to "find their voice" as an artist. Fortunately, this trend is beginning to reverse itself, and our academic institutions are finding a middle ground that equips young artists with the fundamentals AND encourages them to develop their own voices.

POINT OF ART

All art is derived from artists who have come before, to some extent. From this one might be tempted to suggest, both cynically and tritely, that there is nothing new under the sun. While this may be true, I like to believe that originality is not a contrivance but rather the result of study, experience and perseverance. It is a journey into the self, which embraces the cosmic consciousness of those who've gone before us, combined with our own unique life force. Some people are born into this knowledge while for others, it is a lifelong journey, which includes intense introspection and an eagerness to grow and learn. It most certainly involves study. My father said it best, "I'd put my money on the artist with a little less talent who worked hard, before the lazy one with all the talent in the world." Of course, my father also used to sing, "never, never be an artist, if you want roast beef called prime!" Somewhere in the middle, is the potential for each of us to be a fully expressed, professional artist.

Is Life Really All That Boring?

I see it all the time in my young children, those in-between moments that add up to about eighty percent of their waking life. So far they seem to be able to fill them pretty well with exploration and wonder. Will they eventually learn to see them the way grownups do: as boredom?

As adults we won't actually admit to calling them boring, even though that's how we experience them. Teenagers have no problem identifying these moments as boring. Everything is boring to them. As grownups we say we're "chilin' out," "thinking," or "relaxing." We watch TV, wait for people to turn up or something exciting to happen. When on occasion exciting things do happen we instantly forget about all the in-between time we've wasted, waiting for them to happen. We snap into action; we feel alive until boredom sets in once again.

Sure, we all complain about how busy we are, banging our heads against the wall, trying to make ends meet. But are we really more overworked than our ancestors? Is it really possible that we're just marking time, busying ourselves, trying to escape our boredom? Or have we learned as adults to accept the rat race as inevitable.

As children, new to the rules, Danny and Mary don't care about any of this. Nothing is boring to them. How can it be; everything's happening for the first time. Even in their moments of calmness, they seem to be captivated by a serene stillness—we're lucky to have been blessed with extraordinarily good-natured kids. Hopefully, they won't learn to call these in between moments boring, impatient for the next big thing like the rest of us. So far the word hasn't entered their vocabulary. Inevitably it will.

Productive contemplation, introspection, invention, original thinking, intelligent conversation, self-expression seem to have fallen by the wayside in our society. They are the past times of an earlier era, the pursuits one has to be willing to do badly to do well, the ones that often require a mastery of skills or knowledge. "Chillin' out" is our way of filling in for what's missing in our lives. We have instant access to all the wisdom and knowledge of the ages yet most of us would rather "veg" in front of the TV during our "down time."

Time Magazine once did a fascinating spread on happiness, concluding that it requires three things: 1) an ability to create pleasure, 2) an involvement and commitment to our work, relationships, etc and 3) the desire to give meaning to our lives. What if, as adults, we were able to appreciate the newness of every experience, to laugh, to cry, to express an opinion about every moment? What if we threw ourselves into our passions and woke up every day as if we were on a vital mission to change the world? Would we go insane? Probably. Would we upset a lot of people? Definitely. Could we survive in the "real world?" Not without some difficulty.

Yet this describes the life of most of the poets, artists and visionaries I know, who are in the world to question everything others take for granted. The artist's life is not always happy, save for moments of ecstasy when we are rewarded with a creative epiphany. While it's true, being an artist is a restless dance, full of self-examination and uncertainty, at least it's not boring.

On Talking Too Much

The other day a friend took me aside and told me I talk about art too much. Why didn't someone tell me sooner? I could have saved everyone a lot of time and grief. I mean, who wants to be preached at about something we all take for granted as essential to being human. See, there I go again. I just can't help myself.

This was the same friend who also suggested I write an article that never mentions the word art. I thought about what I'd write for an arts column that didn't have anything to do with art. It got me thinking about why I write. I've heard it said that people write about what they know. For me writing is about having something to say, and, since I seem to have so much to say about art, that's what I write about.

I have to admit, I do take this art business awfully serious. I sometimes forget that creativity and self-expression are not the primary pre-occupations of most people. Frankly, I find that hard to imagine. After all, we spend so much time in school learning how to read and write. Why bother? I mean, why go through all that trouble? We're assigned essays and told it's good for us to learn grammar and spelling. We drag our heels, kicking and screaming, "why do I have to write another essay, Mom?"

POINT OF ART

My artistic obsession has taken me on a more political path lately. In addition to my work as a commission portrait artist, I've been doing some advocacy, which is "the process of educating someone else on a specific point of view or facilitating an action in favor of your position." This definition is provided compliments of Marete Wester, from the Michigan Artsletter, published by MACAA. She probably stole it from a dictionary but I thought I'd credit her so she might know at least one person read, with interest, her article called, "Making Advocacy a Habit."

I have in my hands a signed letter from my congresswoman, Carolyn Cheeks Kilpatrick, in which she thanks me for my letter, "encouraging me (her) to cosponsor H.R. 806, a bill that will allow artists and writers who donate their works to take a fair market value deduction on their income tax." She has promised to do just that. As of this writing, that bill is still floating around Congress in need of just a little more advocacy.

Even still, that makes me a powerful advocate for the arts and not just a blowhard who likes to talk about art. Guess what? You too can be an arts advocate. It's fun and it's easy. Just go to http://www.congress.org/congressorg/home/, type in your zip code and let your Congressman know you want them to support this non-partisan bill, which will correct a 40 year old error made when Congress came down on Richard Nixon for deducting his papers to the tune of $400,000. The new law corrects the problems with the old law and prevents abuse. The bill is referred to as the "Heritage Act," because it will encourage professional artists to donate more public art and support local charities. I want to publicly thank Congresswoman Kilpatrick for stepping up to the plate and restoring my faith that someone out there is listening to the cries of artists who have carried this burden far too long.

Well, talk about self-expression. The next time someone says

ROBERT MANISCALCO

I talk too much about art I will simply show him or her my framed letter from my Congresswoman. It's a lovely bunch of words that paint a thousand pictures.

What Is the Point of Art?

I've got a lot of gall. I admit it. When I am asked to juror an exhibition, teach, demonstrate or talk to a group of artists or host a TV show I don't shy away. I see it as another opportunity to spread the word about the transformative power of the arts in our society, our community. I try not to question why I do it anymore. It's important, so I do it. So do a lot of us.

Recently, however, a fellow artist confronted me about what I hoped to accomplish with all this "educating" I'm doing. "After all," he pointed out, "didn't you start out as an artist?" He went on to explain that the job of an artist is "to express a point of view, to satisfy an inner muse, not to educate the public about the value of arts in our lives." Naturally, this got me thinking, a very dangerous pastime indeed.

He was right. This whole thing started from a love of being inside the creative process. I truly love to express myself. I love ideas. I love to invent. I love the contradictions, which are all part of the making and appreciation of great art. After all, it's just my materials and me. I love to throw myself into an invented structure and fly away into the supreme ecstasy of the moment. Who wouldn't?

So why am I doing all this other stuff? When do I get time for me? What art have I done for me lately? I'm so busy writing this book, hosting TV shows, running a gallery, directing plays, managing programs, when do I have time to be an artist? People have even asked me, "when do you find time for a life," as if to say, "get a life."

Ouch!

It's true. Sometimes I get so wound up with all the stuff I'm doing and so caught up in all the questions about why I'm doing it that my head starts to spin.

Then I get to thinking, what if this whole bit I'm doing IS the art? What if my whole life is a work of art? I've always thought of art as a metaphor for life. But what if the opposite is also true? What if life is a metaphor for art? In other words, what if my entire life were one giant work of art in progress?

Everything I know about life I've learned as an artist. Art is not something I do for a living; it is who I am. It is my access to the present and to eternity and to the spiritually unknowable. I can't imagine doing anything else.

And I'm not alone in this passion. Others too, feel their creative life IS their life. And their lives are powerfully lived because they know who they are and what they are doing. Together, we are the creative community and we are the key to a healthy society.

That's why I talk so much about the need for arts. It's a pretty great life. And I live for the day when everyone can find a way to express their humanity instead of negating one another with hatred and wars and the black and white insanity that comes from a life without art.

Don't get me wrong. I'm not saying the arts actually contain *all* the answers to the world's dilemmas. Rather, it is the myriad of questions asked by the artist, which bring us ever closer to the truth. But never close enough to touch it. Art is not a riddle, which always have a specific solution. For instance, how is it possible that an artist can transmit the joy or pain of his/her life through the manipulating of common objects and materials available to everyone? What is it about listening to a Beethoven Symphony that makes being alive somehow more bearable?

We'd have to ask a lot more questions to get to the "Point of Art." The artist is someone who recognizes an amazing thing when it happens and has just enough skill and courage to create the circumstances where its true expression can be allowed to happen. Being an artist is to walk the thin line between order and chaos. The artist must learn to know when to take control and when to give it up. The lessons only great art can teach us, are a requisite for a balanced, fully realized life.

That's why I can't shut up about the arts. That's why I do what I do. Now, if you'll excuse me, I've got some art to make.

Being a Professional Artist

What does it take to become a professional artist—one who makes a living solely through his/her art? There's no question, it's a competitive business—and it is a business, make no mistake about it. You must first realize that to be an artist is to be an entrepreneur, which is a speculative pursuit by nature. You create a work that hopefully someone will want to buy. You must be committed to developing the skills, training and insight to be able to create several bodies of fully resolved artwork that reflect who you are and for which there might be a market. That eliminates about 90% of the people who call themselves "artists." Very few artists are able to make a living from their art. Of course, income is a very narrow criteria for success. Ray MacDonald, defined "The Five Points of Success" as: 1) Visibility 2) Affordability 3) Availability 4) Dependability and 5) Ability.

A lot of artists think they're playing the game of being an artist but amazingly few are really committed to being a professional artist. You might be right to ask, "How do I get in the game?" My answer: keep doing art that feeds your soul, then get off the bench and go find your market. There is no shortage of buyers out there, if you're willing to stop at nothing to find them (marketing) and cultivate them (sales). You don't need to cater to a presumed audience, otherwise known as "selling out." I believe there's a market for anything a serioius artist might produce, if he/she is willing to do what it takes to find it.

Okay, but how do I reach these people in an economical way? One word: Networking. First of all, get a good database and use it. Maintain contact with your past clients. After I have put my soul into creating the best body of work that I can, getting my ego out of the way, I put it out into the world. Now I'm a businessman and my job is service. I help my prospective buyers to own it, install it and show it off. Other services include creating a provenance—a short survey about the artwork, the body of work of which it is a part and a short bio of the artist (with contact information); This can be affixed to the back of the piece.

In some cases I offer clients a discount on the condition that they throw a Vernissage party to unveil and celebrate the recent acquisition—which I always attend. While on the subject of discounts, never offer a reduction in cost unless you are getting something in return. Examples of reciprocal incentives include multiple discounts if all works are purchased together, discounts for paying cash right now, discounts for waiting on delivery, discounts for referrals, etc.

Learn to enjoy the art of closing. What is a close? To close is to ask the prospect to buy the artwork in which they have expressed an interest. Closes draw objections, which opportune further discussion and always end in another close. You can't expect to sell if you don't close.

And don't be afraid to ask past collectors for referrals. Pick 30-40 "a-list" prospects and "warriors" and find reasons to regularly contact them in a personal way by following up now and then with a call, note and/or news clip, "thinking of you." I email an attractive "recent work" announcement to past, current and prospective clients twice a month to keep in regular touch with everyone on my list.

Keep yourself visible to the target group, i.e. past buyers, those known to buy work like yours, those who share the values expressed in your work. This is your market. Expand your circle of influence by getting out and asking people questions. Get into your community.

A good way to do this is to donate to charity auctions. One of the joys of being an artist is to be able to give some of our talent to causes we support. It also can be a great PR and networking opportunity. Make sure you get a free ticket to the event and be prepared to work the room. A word of caution: auctioning off lesser works at charity auctions might drive down your fair market value and have the effect of negative PR. Here's another solution: offer your best work. Tell the charity you want to split the reserve price (the minimum bid). Put a reserve on your work that is just below (10%) your retail/gallery price. Tell them they can keep all of the money above the reserve. It's better to have your best work go unsold at a charity auction than to undermine the efforts of you and/or your dealers. Charities benefit from this system because they get better work from the artists. Also keep in mind the law (as of this writing) stipulates you can only deduct the cost of materials from your taxes and not the fair market value.

Another way to get the word out is to find reasons to attract editorial press. Send press releases containing compelling story ideas, exhibits, workshops, recent commissions and award announcements. Take the time to construct an angle suited to the writer/publication. Give them an "exclusive."

Artists are mavericks by nature. We don't fit easily into the "civilian" community. Galleries and fine arts organizations are of little help in selling your art if you are not willing to go to the matt yourself. Reps don't always represent us best and, as in most other fields, success comes from taking the road less traveled. Successful artists must develop an entrepreneurial spirit to thrive in today's culture. If a love of people is not your thing then you definitely need an agent. If putting yourself in front of people is difficult for you, I say, "get over it." My particular journey led me to open my own gallery in the heart of my community (Grosse Pointe, Michigan), which greatly increased my visibility and stature in the area. I still believe that exhibiting my work alongside other artists built everyone up.

My love of teaching, painting, writing and theatre has lead me to create TV shows on cable and PBS, which actually helped me to become a better artist (I learned so much from my guests). These activities have also led to more sales and commissions. Whatever path your career takes, remember: do what you love and love what you do and you will find satisfaction and happiness. You may even make a few bucks!

Being a Professional Portrait Artist

There are a number of similarities between the way we market fine art and commission portraits. But there are also plenty of exceptions. For those of us who create both I have found myself going after a completely different audience for each genre. For the most part, people who buy art rarely want portraits and vice versa. There are exceptions, of course.

Today there is a lot more competition out there for portraits; more artists are going after the same business. How do each of us get our share of the pie? My answer is to create more pies. I look for and market portraits among groups most likely to buy them, focusing on family portraits rather than butting heads with a hundred other artists competing for the CEO of AT&T. I also scour the business papers for announcements about CEO retirements and awards. I contact family owned businesses.

My family portrait clients all have a few things in common. They are wealthy for the most part. They dote on their children and spouses, usually have a million photographs of them and are looking for the ultimate expression of their love for them. Some have a history of having portraits done in their family. That covers a lot of pie. The point is, there is no shortage of prospects out there, if you're willing to go after them.

Just as with your fine art marketing, your past clients are your richest asset. Make it easy for them to refer you by keeping yourself in front of them and by providing excellent follow up service. Having a portrait is a very personal experience. Treat clients accordingly. After I have painted the best portrait I can possibly paint I help them frame it, varnish it and hang it. Other services include creating a provenance—a short biography of the subject and the artist (with my contact information) to affix to the back of the painting. In some cases I offer them a discount on the condition that they throw a Vernissage (unveiling party) to celebrate the subject(s) of the portrait—which I attend whenever possible.

Discounts should be handled in the same way for any artist. There needs to be reciprocation for a discount to be fair to everyone. Examples of reciprocal incentives include multiple portrait discounts if all portraits are included in the same contract, discounts for starting now, discounts for waiting, discounts for starting "while in the area," discounts for referrals, etc. Learn the art of closing without pressuring your prospects. Don't be afraid to ask past clients for referrals.

Keep in good personal contact with your prospects and "warriors," much the same way you would as a non-commission artist. Expand your circle of influence by getting involved in upscale events. Look for social networking opportunities. One way to do this is to donate small portraits or portrait certificates to charity auctions. As when donating fine art, this can also provide good PR and lead to larger portrait upgrades (money I wouldn't have had otherwise) or to new portrait leads. I have had much better experiences donating portrait certificates than donating my non-commissioned fine art.

Just as with non-commission work, you must find ways to attract editorial press by sending press releases containing anecdotal story ideas as well as exhibit, workshop, commission and award announcements. Take the time to construct an angle suited to the writer/publication. By the way, I have found paid ads a big waste of money—they are a crapshoot at best. They usually target too wide an audience for them to be cost effective. Advertising in a full color, glossy magazine can be prohibitively expensive and it requires a campaign of several consecutive placements to be effective. Find ways to reach out to the community, perhaps as a teacher; be a positive artistic influence. Another way to reach the target group is to join and participate in community organizations. Go beyond arts related organizations, as other artists are not really your target market. Don't be afraid to socialize! There is no substitute for personal contact. These are relatively inexpensive, gratifying techniques that work in the long run. Remember, the network you create over time is your only job security. It must be nurtured if it is to grow.

Portrait artists are mavericks by nature. We don't fit easily into the fine art community; galleries and fine arts organizations are of little help in obtaining commissions—though many offer excellent support like your local art guild or the Portrait Society of America. Reps don't always represent us best and they are usually representing multiple artists. As in most other fields, success comes from taking the road less traveled. If a love of people is among the reasons you went into portraits then it seems to follow that putting yourself in front of people would not be so difficult a stretch.

I believe that exhibiting portraits alongside the non-commission works of yours and other artists builds everyone up.

POINT OF ART

My love of writing, teaching, painting and theatre has lead me to produce a couple instructional videos called "The Power of Positive Painting,"and a novel called, "The Fishfly." These, along with hosting TV shows on cable and PBS, have all helped me to actually create better portraits; I learned so much from my guests. These activities have led to an increase in stature, which has led to more commissions. We all must blaze our own trail. One thing is sure, finding your marketing voice will help lead you to the satisfying and prosperous career we all dream of having.

More About Being a Commission Portrait Artist: Avoid the Common Traps

I marvel at the diverse formative stories of leading portrait artists. I've always felt fortunate to be the son of one of the very best portrait painters of our time, Joseph Maniscalco. I have had the great advantage of learning the ropes from a master artist and a smart businessman. As many of us have discovered, finding a mentor is essential to success. In fact finding a mentor is the first piece of advice I give to anyone starting out in the business. Become an apprentice. Yes, be original, be a maverick but don't waste valuable time reinventing the wheel. Absorb everything you can from someone whose work and career you respect.

In my own career (I started out doing commissions for friends while putting myself through music school when I was nineteen) I have avoided a lot of the common stumbling blocks but not all. These mistakes include accepting commissions when only flat, formless photos were available as reference. Another common practice, one that I want to seriously address, is showing your photos to the client as if they were being asked to choose a wallpaper pattern. In my experience, they simply are too subjective to see how a combination of elements from a variety of images might make for a great portrait. Isn't that what they pay us for, our ability to choose what's essential in creating a work of art? One could argue that after all, we are providing a service. Shouldn't the client get to choose? Also, isn't it better from the artist's standpoint to avoid surprises later? In answer to these two questions I ask: who is really being served when we give up our artistic integrity? The fact is, too many cooks spoil the broth. I'm aware that sharing preliminary photographs or sketches is a widely accepted practice. I just think it's a big mistake. Mistakes like this are the result of the well-intended but misguided desire to please the client.

My alternative is to give myself completely to the client when I'm getting to know them, gathering information and brainstorming with them about what they would like to see in their portrait. I know they are served best when they are able to trust me to create that image for them. I believe the best portrait artists are those who truly love people. Because I do, I know my work will always please the client. I have found that people know when they are in the hands of an artist who both knows what they are doing and cares about the client. If you don't truly care about, aren't fascinated by people then you are definitely in the wrong profession!

The time for collaboration is in the very beginning when discussing the concept and while taking photos. I avoid problems by asking the subject to tell me if I've asked them to pose in a position that feels awkward or uncomfortable. Another time for collaboration is at the end when discussing the funny expression in the corner of the mouth. John Singer Sergeant had it right when he said, "a portrait is a picture of someone with something wrong with the corner of his or her mouth!" Hopefully, you can change these little details to the client's satisfaction without compromising the integrity of the painting. Translating their comments into positive action can really help them to feel like active participants. And nine times out of ten it results in a better portrait.

More advice: never go back and forth between working from life and working from the photo. This only waters down the impact of the final product. No artist can serve two masters. Once I leave the photo(s) I rarely ever go back. Any finishing touches (or corrections) I do from life (or in the case of posthumous portraits from the input of those closest to the subject).

When asked to do more than 3 people in a portrait, I try to convince the client to consider doing several individual portraits instead, suggesting they may be easier to split up when everyone has gone their separate ways. I have reluctantly done as many as eight people in a portrait. Each additional figure multiplies the potential for problems. As incentive, I now charge the same to do eight individual portraits as I do to paint one large group. Believe me it's worth it.

Finally, limit the number of people who can sign off on the painting to just the principals concerned. There is nothing more controversial than a portrait—so don't invite trouble. Most people will respect and go along with this if you stress it. Finding the balance between pleasing the client and protecting the integrity of your art is an ongoing process. I hope this advice is of help.

Note: more tips on being a professional portrait artist can be found on my instructional DVD, "The portrait, a value based system."

Removing the "Ving"
from "Starving Artist"

Like a lot of rustbelt Cities, Detroit has its back against a postindustrial wall. While the arts in Detroit have flourished creatively amid the persisting state of ruin in the city, this intense purity has not tended to put money into the hands of artists. Those with means in Detroit have traditionally suffered from a satellite mentality, which prompts collectors to look to New York or some other destination for the purchase of their cultural treasures. The grass roots are always greener somewhere else. Art buyers are not compelled by what Detroit has to offer. But Detroit's cultural identity must come from within if it is to be authentic, if it is to be embraced, if it is to be truly ours. That will ultimately require Detroit artists and art buyers to come to terms with themselves, zits and all. The same is true in every city. If culture is a reflection of the people, our past, our present, then we, the artists need to make that connection. We can't wave a magic wand over potential buyers and make them suddenly want Detroit art. You can lead a horse to artwork but you can't make him buy. Collectors cannot be counted on to transform the market. I believe that artists are the key to a great society; they are our teachers, our trail blazers. That's why the artists are my heroes. So lets focus on the "star" in starving artist.

That was the point behind my TV series, Art Beat, which ran for two seasons on PBS, Detroit Public TV in Detroit. The show was an insider's look into the process of working artists, revealing how they create the work we see on the walls of Detroit's top exhibition venues. Shot entirely on location, usually in the artist's studio, each half-hour episode spotlighted a local artist whose work was powerful and innovative. Among the artists featured were Robert Sestock, who was one of the original Cass Corridor group, Gilda Snowden, abstract expressionist and Niagra, whose witty sensibility infuses her pop, edgy, urban voice. DVDs of the shows two seasons are available on request.

Of course, the show couldn't fully capture the diversity and depth of the visual art being produced in Detroit. Detroit artists cannot be neatly categorized or compartmentalized. One must experience firsthand the raw creative energy in the new arts spaces that are popping up all over the place. Along with the more established artist enclaves like the Scarab Club, the Pioneer and the Atlas Buildings, new spaces like 4731 Grand River, Brooklyn 2000 are churning out brilliant work by many of Detroit's most groundbreaking artists. Indeed, these are exciting times, creatively, for Detroit.

The challenges of developing an identity for Detroit art, however, is a far trickier proposition, one with which the Detroit Artists Network grappled. The question is: how do you put a face on diversity? Clearly, the abundance of creative energy itself is the chief distinction about which Detroiters can truly brag. But how do those outside Detroit view us? In my travels, I have found most people think of Detroit as raw, chaotic and dilapidated. While not a very attractive combination of adjectives to mainstream tastes, whose idea of a destination is a Caribbean island or an enclosed shopping mall, this image is a source of mystery and wonder to those who appreciate art as a reflection of authentic human experiences. The real Detroit culture has never been the sugarcoated, slick image the PR firms have tried to ease down our throats. Like it or not, Detroit is raw, rude and driven. This rough-hewn image flies in the face of the main stream, which insists on making everything "normal," whatever that is. What makes Detroit great is our diversity, our grit, and our creative will.

Suffice it to say Detroit is not without Star quality artists. What we seem to lack is the confidence and perspective to recognize a good thing when we see it. After all, fine artists will continue to have a hard time being taken seriously when 95% of the population thinks of art as an "accent" in the twinkle of a decorator's eye. It's the serious collectors we want to lure back to Detroit. Collectors will eventually stop importing their art as more Detroit artists commit to ditching the "ving" in "starving artist" and find the courage to become the "Star" professionals they could be.

Art Sales Are Up

Art prices have been skyrocketing in recent years, and I'm not just talking about works by the old masters. Boosted by an influx of Asian buyers keen to Hoover up the classics of the modernist canon, sales at Sotheby's and Christie's in London continue to break records. Assigning value to art is a tricky business, especially in the long term, because by far the most important factor in making art works valuable is what experts say and write about them. Retail sales of art and "wall décor" (whatever that is) topped $35.3 billion in 2002, a 14% increase from 2000. And the trend is continuing. This, according to a survey funded by the Art Publisher's Association. The study determined consumers tend to fall into one of two categories. Art connoisseurs, make up over one-quarter of the total art market, consisting of "affluent and highly educated baby boomers who view themselves as collectors for whom decorating takes a back seat." The other group consists mainly of home decorators, who make up 28% of the market. These are "largely budget-minded young marrieds who have a need to buy art to fill empty walls in new homes," says Pam Danziger, president of Unity Marketing and author of the book, "Why People Buy Things

POINT OF ART

They Don't Need." The reasons for mentioning these statistics found in a 2004 article from ART BUSINESS NEWS, are two fold. First, to point out something I've been saying all along: fine art is a multi-billion dollar business and second, to have an excuse to examine whether serious art by local artists can also be collectable art. The more I dig into the workings of the Detroit art market the more appalled I am at the pervasive attitudes of the starving artist set. I am far more impressed by those few artists who have something important to say through their art, and are reaching out to and the collectors who are responding. There are a handful of talented artists who don't see bearing their soul in their work and selling it as mutually exclusive.

Don't get me wrong, I'm not suggesting artists should cave into market pressures and only produce art they think will sell. "The personal connection with the art takes precedence over whether it fits a particular space on the wall," says Danziger. I have found that serious art is very desirable and sellable. Sure, Detroit is a tough market but this expression of powerlessness, so deeply entrenched in the Detroit art culture, is serving no one. The solution lies in the hands of the artists. We have to stop bashing buyers. All we can do is try to educate the market.

Art consultant, Katherine Carter, provides a great bottom line: "Accepting the responsibility of promoting your work and determining your destiny, by controlling the quality and frequency of your promotions and capitalizing on the resources that are available through marketing research, and public relations and communications experts requires a major commitment. These actions provide the professional artist with the power to become a formidable player and a serious stake holder in the outcome."

To me, selling art, whether as a publicly funded installation or as a free standing work of art, is, in a way, a completion of the creative process. It is as much a part of the delivery of the idea as the materials themselves. That is not to say that it is not "art" unless someone buys it. I have seen enough masterpieces returned to the artist at the end of an exhibit to know that selling is not the primary criteria for a great work of art or a successful show. On the other hand, I've never met an artist who wasn't happy when he/she sold a work for a fair price.

And let's not forget the collector, who has the privilege of drawing inspiration from the work on a daily basis. Most agree, it's a very addictive hobby. They have a responsibility for sharing their pride in ownership, participating in the effective presentation and provenance of the work. They are invested in the career of the artist. It's a sacred trust.

So where are all these art buyers? After all, $35.3 billion is a lot of money. I believe, perhaps naively, that every serious work of art has a buyer, if we have the skill and tenacity to find him/her. Potential art buyers are everywhere. It's a fairly wide demographic. Certainly, anyone who shows up at a gallery must be considered fair game. Getting them there is a continuing challenge. Learning the tactful art of selling is extremely important for a successful career. It's a thrill to be there when a work of art does find its owner. It's like watching someone fall in love. I look forward to the day when the serious art community steps up to the plate and claims its share of that $35 billion.

Stop Supporting the Arts

With the closing of several prominent galleries across the country, the question arises, "what does it mean to support the arts?" I sometimes talk about the need for supporting the arts as if our humanity hung in the balance, which incidentally, it does. The trouble is we tend to present the idea of support as a sacrifice, a burden to carry, like eating our vegetables. We call it "serious" art and beg people to tolerate it. Then we're surprised when they'd rather spend a quiet evening around the TV.

I spend a lot of time trying to convert those who might like the water if only they dared to drink. After all, I've experienced first-hand the transformative power of the arts, so I have a deep faith people will eventually wake up and smell the turpentine. I'm proud that first time collectors purchased about 40% of the artworks sold at my gallery.

On the other hand, there isn't a whole lot one person can do to support the arts. The arts community starts with the individual. Not everyone chooses to afford art, even with all the excellent values among emerging artists. We can't expect people to attend the art openings, concerts, poetry readings, fund raisers, etc. going on all the time. Maybe we should take attendance. Maybe we should have a cardpunch like they do at Starbucks. Ten concerts and you get a free cup of coffee. People often tell me I'm preaching to the choir. I'm well aware that if you're reading this you probably don't need an incentive to be inspired. So listen up choir: you are officially absolved of any obligation to support the arts. Stop doing it. It's not working, so quit. The charity bit will no longer be required. Thank you very much.

There, now doesn't that feel better. Let's just "veg" in front of the TV for a while and imagine a world where other people derive sustenance from the arts, not because they should but because they want to. Not you. You and I are finished with all that running around, chasing artistic epiphanies like so many broken dreams. Let the others take over for a while.

It reminds me of the book, "Atlas Shrugged," by Ayn Rand, where all the movers and shakers suddenly stop compensating for the "others," the ones who talk the talk but don't walk the walk. What if atlas shrugged? What if the network went down? What if the choir refused to sing?

Well, for one thing it would be pretty quiet. Arts programs would fall flat on their face, more galleries would close and after a while people would begin to complain that their lives were kind of dull. But because there were no artists to lead the way they wouldn't really know what to do about it so they'd begin to fight with their spouses, just to keep from going insane. Eventually, whole communities would rise against one another and even entire nations. And certain people would rise up, using fear and ignorance to control the masses who've found no meaning in their lives but who know they need to fight to protect their ideologies.

Sound familiar?

The fact is we've long abandoned the arts as a vital form of nourishment and the cost to our society is the dull aching feeling that something is missing but we don't know exactly what it is. It's called JOY, and it comes from participating in the creative process. And if you and I don't wake up to that fact soon it may be too late. It's not that others aren't supporting the arts. It's us, the ones who feel it needs to be supported in the first place. We don't need their support. As of this moment, I'm finished trying to spoon feed arts and culture to them. If they're content with BMWs and granite counter tops and plasma TVs then so be it. Let's you and I hog all the arts for ourselves, what do you say? Let's not ruin our fun by trying to reach civilians about what's going on in our community. Let's not give them the satisfaction of knowing what they're missing. Don't share this article with anyone. Don't tell anyone about your personal experiences with the arts, certainly don't share any more epiphanies. Let's just sit back and enjoy the ride. It's a tough job but someone's got to do it.

Can Your Kid Really Do It?

Occasionally I hear the statement, "my kid could do that" in reference to abstract or, so called, "modern" art. So let's explore the question of whether your kid really can paint like Picasso or say, De Kooning. My answer to the "my kid could do that" statement is "yes" and "no." Yes, only a child is capable of the kind of inner freedom expressed by these great modern masters. And no: most people, including children, lack the tenacity and open heartedness necessary to give themselves over to the creative process. The "my kid" comment is irritating on so many levels because it trivializes the work of serious artists, many of whom have devoted their entire lives to the search for their own voice.

What's worse is the superficial attempt. We all know the hackneyed amateurs, who casually pick up a brush or step onto the stage, surprised when the world doesn't fall to their knees in awe of their natural talent. Their delicate egos long since crushed whatever native gifts they may have had. These people are every bit as insulting as the "my kid" crowd.

The fact is, very few people have what it takes to be a professional artist. Fine painters, musicians, actors, poets, dancers, etc. are a rare breed indeed. They must be intensely dedicated, extraordinarily savvy—not to mention supremely talented—to make it as a professional. The arts are not a good career choice for those with a weak constitution.

Despite the common myths about "crazy" artists, successful artists are some of the most grounded individuals I have ever met. Ironically, whenever professional artists, musicians and poets get together they rarely talk about art. They're usually discussing business models and marketing strategies and coming up with ways to support a family, just like any other entrepreneur.

Meanwhile, the media is heavily promoting the idea that anyone can make art. Michael H. Margolin, former Executive Director of the Wayne County Council for Arts, History and Humanities, points out that we are seeing more and more television segments about how easy it is to "decorate" your home with cute little "accent pieces" you can make yourself in minutes.

Martha Stewart is the first person to come to mind. Margolin believes these shows "do a great disservice to the artist, putting their work in the same context as framed feathers and other froufrou." Margolin feels this is another salvo, unwittingly fired, against the visual arts. "These design pieces, whether they are good or mediocre, are unfailingly referred to by the designer, the team and the program host as "art", therefore blurring the distinction between a design used to supplement a decorating scheme and a work of art growing out of personal conviction, intellectual concerns, and emotional impulses. The person who sits before a canvas and pours out heart, soul, skill on a painting meant to exist in the hopes of communicating an idea or emotional state-whether good, bad, or in-between is an artist." Can a craft be art? Rarely. When it rises above the cookie-cutter level to something expressing the original thoughts and feelings of an individual; this is when it begins to enter the realm of fine art.

There's another important distinction that needs to be made between the arts professional and the amateur, those noble souls who produce art purely for the love of creating. There are many wonderful artists who aren't in it for the money. This doesn't mean they aren't excellent or pure it just means they are not actually professional. Many of our most serious artists fall into this category. Being an amateur is not a bad thing. It's when the ego gets to be bigger than the talent that there's a problem.

So when I encourage person to be self-expressed I'm not suggesting he become a charlatan. Pursuit of an artistic muse may mean different things to different people. For some it means fun time for their child between serious studies of reading and math. To others, it is a spiritual quest, a profound attempt to answer the questions of our existence. For many of us, it's also the way we earn a living. It is a noble profession. Integrity is key.

So how do we approach art as a profession? Are there professional standards for artists, as in the legal or say, plumbing professions? Not really. The path to becoming a professional artist is varied indeed. While doctors have a clear career track, with clearly defined benchmarks along the way, artists usually are the result of a unique life arch.

What do professional visual artists have in common? They often have received professional arts training or been apprenticed with established professionals, while some are considered "outsider" artists, having no training whatsoever. Professional artists often win awards, grants or fellowships. Their works are in prominent collections. They have developed an established fair market value over time. Galleries often represent them, although many professionals prefer to remain unaffiliated. They may have ties to academia. They may be members of professional arts organizations. They have achieved recognition or critical acclaim in the media. They may have published articles documenting their careers. They may have established some degree of notoriety. They usually will have professional tools such as resumes, biographies, artist statements, portfolios, catalogues, websites, etc.

One thing is certain, artists must think outside the box, when it comes to making a living. But there are many criteria for success, only one of them being money. Making a living solely as an artist is a worthwhile pursuit. Creativity is your capital. If the satisfaction of creating is its own reward, marketing your art is at times challenging, but necessary. Taking a stand against mediocrity and mendacity is a good first step. But a serious career as an artist requires talent, hard work and tenacity. It must also include taking oneself seriously as a professional. I'd love to see your kid do that.

The "It" of Art

A couple years back the Detroit Artists Network met to discuss ways to promote Detroit artists. The question came up: what is the "it" of Detroit art? Most cities have asked themselves a similar question. Is there a predominant genre or movement arising from the tremendous creative energy that is pulsing in every corner of our city? It seems a harmless enough question. After all, we are just trying to find ways to increase awareness within our community (and globally) that Detroit is home to several world-class visual artists who are producing work in search of a market to support it.

Detroit art has begun to be recognized internationally. But what is Detroit art? Clearly, we have a musical voice in Detroit with Motown and Techno. And yes, the Cass Corridor movement represents a clear, historical precedent for visual art. But what have we done lately? How might we characterize the current Detroit art scene?

The very idea of trying to define the "it" of art is so abhorrent to most artists that it came as no surprise when the conversation hit a brick wall. Artists are the last people to ask about marketing their own work, let alone the work of an entire community. That's the reason we have galleries, reps, consultants, and in a larger context, arts councils, associations and agencies. Part of their job is to define the market. The marketing process, by definition, implies an attempt to respond to demand, to exploit a niche, i.e. making paintings with wine bottles, because wine tasting is in vogue. There is a fundamental disconnect between the artist and his or her market that inhibits him or her from dealing with marketing. I think this is as it should be. After all, at what point does the artist cross the line between expressing his or her most personal thoughts and feelings and pandering to the lowest common denominator? I refer to one artist, who after years of pandering to the market selling "wine" art, made a dramatic turnaround and is having much more success marketing a new series of more serious art.

To a great extent, the artist must remain detached from his/ her market, especially during the conception and execution. But that doesn't mean artists should bury their heads in the sand. The challenge for artists is to study the demographics; what groups might buy his or her work? I believe, perhaps naively, that there is a market for every work of art that is sincerely conceived, if one is willing and able to find it. Artists need to think outside the box. If your work is about cars, put your work in front of car lovers, who may not have, heretofore, considered collecting art.

Dealing with marketing is essential to the life of a professional artist. Branding a community is another issue altogether. The conversation breaks down as we turn our attention to developing a slogan or mission that attempts to characterize or somehow express the creative energy of ALL artists in any given market, like Detroit. Can it be done? Is there an "It factor" for the Detroit arts scene? There are plenty of excellent models in other regions. In the Lowcountry of South Carolina, for example, marsh scenes, painted au plein aire have a ready market. In some regions the "it of art" evolves naturally over a period of years. Other regions, like Detroit, seem to prefer ambiguity. Detroit art, it would seem, defies description.

But let's give it a try. There seems to be a preponderance of found object art, perhaps a metaphor for the dilapidation confronting the city. There is also a lot of pop art floating around. I've noticed a lot of expressionistic cityscapes. But that's the trap. The "it" of art cannot be found in any one genre. What we need is a slogan—something that says it all in one neat phrase! One slogan suggested for Detroit by Jenenne Whitfield was: "Detroit, the city of originality." That still doesn't get to the heart of what Detroit art is all about. How about, "Detroit, city of broken bottles?" I better stop before I get in real trouble.

We know how to break an artwork down to its visual and conceptual elements. But what is it that makes some artwork literally jump off the walls? We, as artists, are hard-pressed to define our individual "it," let alone our collective "it."

How then, will we ever find "it?" It's like trying to find Kansas from Oz.—so simple yet so very difficult. Clearly, we need regular, intelligent art criticism in our media to explore the "it" of Detroit's arts scene. Having a critic not only would generate interest in the art of Detroit it would also help highlight movements and make connections among regional art forms. Without consistent, objective criticism, Detroit collectors will continue to be left fending for themselves and buying Detroit art will remain a crapshoot.

As in most healthy art centers, Detroit needs a strong gallery system. We need to revive the Detroit Art Dealers Association (DADA). We need a comprehensive, easily accessible source for upcoming gallery information. One of DADA's first orders of business would be to produce a brochure, listing galleries in and around Detroit, available at places like the airport. The bottom line is that the arts community needs to participate in the branding of its own market. It is a process not just of identification but of building confidence and integrity in our business practices, individually and as a community. That's where "it" will have to start.

Should the Government Fund the Arts?

With the economy stagnating and huge deficits looming it has once again become fashionable to cut arts funding. Clearly, we have some serious problems; across the board cuts are something we all must endure. My only objection is that the arts have once again become the poster child for fiscal excess. The fact is that arts funding, even in good times, is such a small fraction of the entire budget that any funding cuts have little real effect on the bottom line. Nonetheless, arts and culture have traditionally made a tempting target. After all, why should hard working citizens pay for the elite's creative time? Maybe I'm being overly dramatic, but it's still a very important and difficult question.

The trend toward moving arts support to the private sector is an earnest attempt to resolve the issue. Such a transition makes a great deal of sense. Arts funding should not be looked at as an "extra" or as "pork." If it came down to choosing between roads and bridges or grants to arts and cultural endeavors what would you do? My response is to suggest that there is no point in building a house if you don't plan to include heat, water, perhaps a refrigerator and some furniture. The arts fill the domicile of who we are. Creativity and inspiration are so fundamental to our existence that we actually forget they are all around us. They are the stories we tell when we get home from work, the lessons we learn from lost love, the memories of our mother's caress. Most people take the aesthetics of their lives for granted. Those who are not exposed to the arts grow up with a huge hole in their soul. The unique way each of us expresses ourselves, moment to moment, gets to the heart of being alive. It's what drives us and we are what drive the economy.

But still, after all the arguments in favor of bringing art into our lives, is it really the government's responsibility to provide arts funding? I used to own a commercial art gallery, which was driven by the market. I am also past president of the Wayne County Council for Arts, History & Humanities, a non-profit organization which currently derives 80% of its funding from government sources. Different economic forces motivate each type of organization (commercial and non-profit). Yet each plays an important role in a healthy cultural life.

A few years ago, a handful of entrepreneurs, such as myself, opened a number of for-profit galleries that were not dependent upon local, state or federal funding. The idea that developing a healthy artists market, one that is not subsidized by tax dollars, that is market driven, is very appealing. It carries a certain capitalistic idealism. Just like any other part of our economy, artists and galleries must be responsive to the real market, not some made up utopia. The only problem with this very sensible model is that there is no room for error. If the work doesn't sell the gallery goes out of business.

But again, why should society care about a bunch of folks throwing paint around, anyway? The real question, in terms of our culture, is where do we develop new ideas? How do people learn about their creative potential? What do people of other cultures do when they're afraid, in love, confused? Where will our comfortable worldview be challenged? Where's the space for experimentation? How is our intellectual, spiritual growth to be nurtured? If all we have are artists trying to satisfy the market, what will eventually become of our society? What will become of us? The list of words that come to mind include stagnation, apathy, sterility, uniformity, atrophy, anger, intolerance, bigotry, chauvinism and xenophobia.

Don't get me wrong; I firmly believe there is a tremendous, untapped market for art that is challenging, controversial and mind-expanding—work that is produced by serious artists. Can fine art be both serious and marketable? Clearly we cannot rely solely on the market to produce the educational opportunities that our non-profit arts organizations are attempting to provide.

Should the corporate sector pitch in extra to make our world a better place to live by providing arts funding? Of course. Will they? Based on the moral vacuum demonstrated by corporate scandals and hostile takeovers, I tend to doubt it. Even Bill Gates has an eye out for the PR value of his generosity. We don't hate Microsoft the way we once did, do we? The private sector is fundamentally motivated by profit. This is not meant as an indictment; it's just the way it is. We need to appreciate the distinct and important roles the corporate/commercial and the non-profit sectors must play in a healthy society.

The conversation around arts funding is too important for art spirits to become polarized, purists on one side and "sell-outs" on the other. Finger pointing and snobbery is what keeps the arts isolated from society. Most people have no idea where their art tax dollars are going, let alone why on earth they might want to experience live theatre or actually buy a work of art. It's hard to expect public support for something with which most people have scant experience or understanding. Artists and arts organizations have to roll up their sleeves and reach out to where the people live. We need to commit ourselves to finding a common ground where a healthy arts community can thrive, despite changing fashions and fortunes.

It's Time for a
Strong Gallery System

In the previous essay, "Should government support the arts," I explored some of the positive roles the private and public sectors can play in a healthy arts market. I thought I had made a compelling argument. In response a few readers still insisted that the arts should survive only in the open market and not be supported by the government under any circumstances. Pete Waldmeir, of the Detroit News, framed government support for arts as a veiled effort to "saddle taxpayers with expenses to support our hobbies." One artist present proclaimed artists should "rise up with dignity and make our own way as other professions do." Rather than rehashing the debate over the importance of government funding for the arts, I thought we might focus on how serious fine artists might actually go about holding their own in the real world economy.

Let's take another good, hard look at the fine art market here in Detroit. Comparatively speaking, the retail value of art is lower here than in other comparable cities and much lower than in healthier models such as Santa Fe or Chicago. One would think this were great news for art collectors, who should, one would expect, be flocking to Detroit to pick up on all the great bargains. After all, where else can you find world-class talent producing compelling, original artwork for under $500? Could it be that Detroit has glutted the market with so much great art that the supply has simply exceeded demand? No, it's not quite that simple. So where is the breakdown occurring?

In other essays I have railed about the many scams out there, taking business away from local artists. For example, we are now beginning to hear about lawsuits brought by galleries representing the prints of Thomas Kinkade. These galleries are complaining that Kinkade's company is undercutting agreed upon retail prices and selling cheaper images to Walmart and other chains. It remains to be seen whether consumers will continue to "invest" as much as $5,000 for touched up prints of sentimental landscapes by this most popularly appealing marketer. His is a multi-million dollar empire. But it's only the tip of the iceberg. Suffice it to say, the commercial fine art business is a thriving industry—no need for charity there.

So, who is "supporting" this multi-billion dollar industry; who are all these "shallow" art buyers? Is all our "serious art" really going over peoples' heads or are there other forces at work? And why should legitimate artists and dealers care about this Reader's Digest constituency, anyway? More to the point, how can serious, local artists get a piece of this action without compromising their integrity? Sadly, legitimate artists are shutting themselves out of the extremely lucrative fine art market because they refuse to play by the rules of supply and demand, leaving the market open to charlatans and savvy opportunists like Thomas Kinkade.

So let's back up a minute. Rather than looking down our noses and blaming these marketers, let's see what we can learn from their successful models. What has Thomas Kinkade been doing that has made him so successful? Successful marketing requires organization. Kinkade has controlled the supply of his work, generated demand by developing incentives for his galleries and backed them up with an effective advertising campaign. He has thoroughly researched and targeted his market like a laser beam. He has essentially branded his style and effectively packaged and merchandised his product to the public.

How can serious artists do that and still have time to create? Until we have an effective gallery system in place Detroit artists will continue to flop around in the marketing void. But alas, Detroit artists simply do not support a gallery system, never have. Even though it's clear that in communities with a strong gallery system the fine art market is thriving. This is not to say Detroit doesn't have some great galleries. We do. But predominantly, Detroit's art scene consists of pockets of makeshift art spaces. We have incredible arty parties, beer fests, and spontaneous happenings. We are enjoying a grassroots explosion of talent pushing up through the pavement, appearing at nightclubs and free alternative spaces all over town. We are cool. We are hip. We are clever. We are culturally aware and artistically deep. But, let's face it, serious collectors aren't buying all the hype.

Sure, there will always be a few artists who will inevitably do extremely well in any environment because they are determined to do so. They have found and filled their niche. But for the most part, Detroit artists suffer under the delusion that their only problem is packaging. They seem to by saying, "maybe if we looked hipper we would be taken more seriously by the art consumer." This is an egregious in-authenticity.

The problem isn't packaging; the problem is that Detroit artists are literally inaccessible to Detroit art buyers. Sure, an artist may turn up in a restaurant for a while, then a couple months later, at an art fair, then in a juried exhibition. He/she may even make an appearance at one of our hip art galleries but then, inevitably, disappear for a while. Collectors may take the initiative to follow the artist, if they can keep up. Those artists, and I'm talking about some of the best artists in Detroit, who choose to remain unaffiliated with a commercial gallery are deluding themselves if they think they can thrive by arranging the occasional studio visit or developing a following with the periodic exhibit, here and there. It's the first rule of marketing: the buyer must have access to the product—physically and aesthetically. It's no wonder most of the top Detroit galleries prefer to work with non-local talent.

And it's the primary reason why they work with the same few artists on an exclusive, ongoing basis. They are in control of the supply. The artist can only be accessed through them. Artists need a continuous presence. Websites come to mind. A great Website, however, is not the same as having an actual presence in the market. At best a Website is a placeholder. It may even whet the appetite and provide contact information for further exploration on the part of the buyer. But so far, no one has come up with a Website that can compete with the actual experience of standing before an actual work of art next to an expert dealer or better yet next to the artist himself. Worst of all, the artist Website contributes nothing to the real issue: the development of a buying community or art market.

The way for Detroit to develop an effective art market is for us to begin practicing basic marketing skills. Professional artists need to develop consistently high standards of excellence in their work, build and commit to a consistent retail value of their work, brand their work by developing a distinct style and body (or bodies) of work, control the availability of their work (glutting the market may be Kinkade's ultimate downfall), provide a logical range of prices, comparing values of like artists work, be continually accessible to the public during business hours (galleries are handy for that), develop a deep understanding of the market (know the demographics of the people who will likely buy their work), actively participate in the promotion of their work by devising and investing in an effective PR campaign, and expand their circle of influence inside and outside the their market area.

Keep in mind, it's a waste of time trying to squeeze water from a rock. The most important marketing skill, however, is to be consistent and fair in all business dealings, backing the work up with integrity. As simple as this last part sounds, I assure you, it is most uncommon.

Galleries need to step up to the plate as well. Art dealers need to become the champions of the artists they were meant to be. Commercial galleries are not nightclubs nor are they the grazing troths of the elite. They need to be the place where people can go to see, learn about and collect fine art; the consumer must be able to trust the gallery to exhibit artwork that moves, touches and inspires them. We can no longer afford to be party to the revolving door practices of a failed model. I'm speaking primarily to the latest outcrop of "commercial" galleries, who are anxious to mount exciting exhibits without any commitment to the artists they're exhibiting. This revolving door policy just isn't working. Galleries have to be willing to commit to their artists and groom collectors to buy their work. The more established galleries have already learned this lesson. They actually represent their artists.

We need to encourage open, honest dealings within our community. The fine arts community has to be willing to stop the catch 22 of mistrust, once and for all. The status quo will no longer suffice. Unless we work together we will continue to flounder.

122

POINT OF ART

But what about all those people buying BMWs and granite counter tops instead of serious art? Certainly, there is a tremendous learning curve in educating the public about appreciating the value of owning fine art, not merely as a decorative element or status symbol but as a vital part of their way of being. Brow beating the consumer is not the answer. We must remember wealth does not necessarily go hand-in-hand with cultural literacy. We must always be teaching. Decorative art rarely survives the redecoration process, whereas true art is eternal. An effective art dealers association would help in reaching this untapped market. But we must accept that there will always be those who feel more comfortable matching a cheap print or a knockoff to their sofa rather than venturing into the realm of one-of-a-kind, original artwork that feeds the soul. We certainly have our work cut out for us.

This kind of education, incidentally, should be the primary mission of most governmental arts & culture agencies. As I said in other essays, the non-profit sector needs to be working in tandem with the commercial sector. If we truly want arts and culture to thrive in our community non-profits must focus on matching and/or replacing decreasing government funds with alternative private sources for essential programs and services. Meanwhile, we must also commit to building an effective commercial market for Detroit artists, able to hold its own in the real world. A strong gallery system is the key.

The Art of Professionalism

Few experiences give me more satisfaction than being part of the excitement and awe of another human being responding to an invitation to enter the world of an artist through his/her work. It's a miraculous communion—one that needs to be celebrated and nurtured. For this reason, I can't think of anything I'd rather be than a professional artist, art dealer and arts advocate. It's very easy to quip that art is just another business, when really it is so much more.

As a professional artist/dealer, I derive my sole income from the sale of art. By this simple definition of "professional," it would be very tempting for artists and dealers to forsake the goal of making great art in favor of producing only what is marketable— many do. It is, after all, the definition of marketing to tailor production to what will most likely sell (selling is trying to convince someone to buy something they didn't know they wanted). True success, however, is when an artist's market and his/her product are in harmony. It is the age-old search for one's dharma— our true gift to the world. The art profession, then, is more than a livelihood; it is an expression of our connection with humankind. I believe art, made and marketed with integrity, is one of the greatest gifts a creative person can share with the world. In this sense, profit is the measure of the artist's contribution to humanity. As a community, we need to take a stand for developing a standard for excellence in both the creating and selling of art.

I place a high premium on originality—I want to see the hand of the artist. Rubber stamps just don't do it for me; for me, mass production is the antithesis of art. I value a deep understanding and intimacy of the craft, a full resolution of ideas and a mastery of materials. I admire those who courageously respond to their world through their art—free of ego and pretension. I want to believe in the work. I want it to teach me something about being human and I shouldn't need a PhD in art history to understand it—even though it may help. I want it to connect me with my past, present and future.

In the world of contemporary art (living artists) the quality of the work, the stature of the artist (gallery/museum shows, notoriety, awards, collections, provenance of works, etc) and the fair market value of the artist's work (what it has sold for in the past) determine the prices an artist may charge. Artists are a good long-term investment if their work is of consistently high quality and if the artist has proven he/she is on a solid career track. There needs to be a documented relationship between value and price.

For some reason, I have found that many emerging collectors need to be empowered to trust (and to deepen) their own tastes when it comes to choosing art. Sadly, I once attended an art auction (on a cruise ship) where, in frustration that sales were slow, the auctioneer presented a painting with its back to the audience—we couldn't see the piece. Amazingly, more people felt comfortable bidding on what they couldn't see than on what they had seen earlier with their own eyes. This disturbing episode brought home for me the central in-authenticity eating away at our fine art market: misinformation and cynicism coming from those who are in the unique position to know and teach the public about fine art—our local galleries and art dealers. Buying art requires a great trust, which must be earned, not squandered for a fast buck.

The Whistle Blower—an Exposé

There are a number of marketing practices in the art-world, which simply do not stand up to the light of day. One inauthenticity that compromises the integrity of the legitimate retail art market is the big business of presenting mass-produced "starving-artist" paintings as originals. I'm talking about assembly-line art, usually imported in bulk from third world countries, placed in large, elaborate, foam blown frames. They are usually "oldish" looking paintings with subjects like little girls on swings, Roman ruins or conventional florals. They are intended to fill walls, no more, no less. These knockoffs and/or mass produced copies are signed with fictitious names and no acknowledgment to the original works. Paintings like these are available at a very low cost through numerous international distributors and marked up as much as 10 to 15 times their original cost. While some of these galleries are candid about the origins of these products, many are not. I have experienced first-hand where dealers have claimed these knockoffs as having been painted by "undiscovered artists from Europe" and acquired as a result of "extensive travels abroad." Let's be frank, there will always be a place for "starving artists" paintings and "knock offs" but there will never be a case in favor of pretense or subterfuge regarding the provenance (information about who painted it, where it has shown, etc.) of a work of art.

Another common practice of certain galleries is to inflate the prices of limited edition prints, selling them as "savvy" financial investments. Cruise ships often hold art auctions. We took a cruise a few years back. I stopped in on an auction where the auctioneer (a representative of a large gallery in the northwest suburbs of Detroit) compared buying a Salvador Dali limited edition print to investing in Microsoft during its infancy. Please! Just because a gallery prints a "letter of authenticity" doesn't necessarily mean the image is authentic. Most Dali prints floating around are not authentic. There are no government regulations regarding claims of authenticity so we are at the mercy of the art dealers themselves. And despite all the hype, a Thomas Kinkade print is unlikely ever to appreciate in value. In 2006, an arbitration panel ruled against the so-called "Painter of Light." The dealers and ex-dealers allege that Kinkade used his religious beliefs—and manipulated theirs—to induce them to invest in Thomas Kinkade Signature Galleries, independently owned stores licensed to deal exclusively in his work. They also allege that they were stuck with inventory they couldn't sell, forced to open additional stores in markets that could not sustain them; they were undercut by discounters that sold Kinkade prints at prices they were forbidden to match. And they accuse the artist of scheming to devalue Media Arts Group before he took the company private for $32.7 million in early 2004, renaming it Thomas Kinkade Co.

Clearly, we need to set higher standards regulating the print market, especially with all the new technologies on the market. Legitimate, quality printmaking is an expressive media that should be protected and regulated.

Perhaps the most heartbreaking of these dubious marketing practices is the existence of art "sweatshops." Certain art dealers are taking advantage of illegal immigrants, paying them below minimum wage, to copy other artists' work, literally ripped from the pages of Art in America, signing fictitious names and selling them to local corporations and private collectors for ten times what they're paying their artists. This is a big business and it is happening in many communities across the country.

Less serious, yet perhaps one of the biggest stumbling blocks to Detroit's bourgeoning fine art market, is what one art dealer called our "wild, wild west" mentality. Metro Detroit artists have little solidarity with one another and almost none with their commercial galleries. Sadly, aside from the amazing depth and availability of exceptional talents, what distinguishes our city from healthier art markets is that Detroit artists feel they have the right, indeed obligation, to show their work wherever and whenever they can or want. While it's true, it is a free country; it is also true this practice just doesn't work. At one time, artists would show at my gallery, only to turn up two months later at a restaurant down the street or another gallery across town, varying prices, according to how much commission the venue "took." In any functioning, thriving art market, this practice would be considered grounds to blacklist an artist. In Detroit, it's business as usual.

Detroit artists justify this practice by arguing they need the exposure when in fact it only devalues their work, their reputations, not to mention the venues in which they show. It's really very simple: value is directly related to supply. No matter how fine the work, flooding the market and not keeping consistent retail prices creates confusion and lowers values. This "revolving door" policy is the single reason Detroit supports only a tiny handful of professional artists and galleries.

This is not to say restaurants, clubs, associations and other alternative spaces shouldn't play a role in exposing and developing new talent. Detroit's unique artistic contribution, however, is being squandered when our best artists flit around from flower to flower, art space to art space. Still, there is a long tradition, even pride, in this ineffective, freewheeling, "guerrilla" marketing method. Detroit artists deserve better. One solution: if an artist is that prolific, he or she might establish relationships with galleries and exhibition venues in other regional centers as well. That's how artists establish national reputations and raise the value of their work.

Artists, galleries, art centers, councils, guilds/clubs, schools and alternative venues must come together to determine how they each can contribute to a common good. Until then, serious art collectors will continue to look elsewhere to buy their art—or worse, languish in apathy. Meanwhile, many legitimate, gifted artists (and venues) must continue fighting for survival in this gray market. Detroit is enjoying an upsurge of interest in the arts. The potential market is poised and ready. Are we, the artists? Let's not let these ridiculous practices stand in the way of Detroit becoming the international art center it deserves to be. I do not accept the cynical notion of the "starving artist" or that Detroiters are "blue-collar" and therefore not interested in culture. That's just too absurd for words.

It's up to our art schools, guilds, commercial galleries, nonprofit spaces, agencies, councils and alternative venues to provide leadership and a commitment to the arts community. We simply can no longer afford to stand by and allow the art market to be handled like a college food fight. If we artists want to be taken seriously by the larger community we need to develop professional standards and some modicum of solidarity.

What's the moral of the story?

Could we as a community benefit by valuing creativity and professionalism a little more? Sure. Do we need to be diligent as we work together collectively for a healthy arts community? Definitely. It took me sometime, as a gallery owner, to learn things about the art business I sometimes wish I didn't know. What keeps me going are the little epiphanies along the way, when a person invests in themselves by purchasing their first original artwork or discovers a new way of looking at the world. I believe people are willing to pay for quality and integrity.

We can't be afraid to take a close, hard look at ourselves. Sugar coating the truth and burying our heads in the sand won't cut it anymore. We all must take responsibility if we really want a healthy art scene. My hope is that conversations such as these will encourage more dialogue and lead to changes in these dubious practices. Clearly there is a need and a commitment within our community to come together for the common good and I am confident the results will be powerful. I say again and again, we need a fully functioning Detroit Art Dealers Association to deal with the issue of exclusivity, among many others. We need forums to educate artists and arts venues about professional marketing and the roles each of us can play in creating an even playing field. We need to ask questions. For instance, how should the mission of a nonprofit exhibition space differ from that of a commercial gallery? We need to generate communication and abundance instead of cynicism.

Who knows, it may lead to my walking into someone's home and discovering an inspiring work of art graces the wall—a work of art to which the homeowner is passionately attached. We will stay up late talking and learning more about life and one another than we ever dreamed possible. That kind of success is very satisfying. To me, that's what this business is all about.

The Gift of Culture

I think there are still those among us who believe culture refers to those fancy folks who are trying to outdo each other's mink coats at "The Theatre" (please read with a bad British accent). My goal today is to do what I can to dispel this silly idea once and for all. As many of us now know, culture is that important part of our lives that keeps us in touch with who we are. I would go so far to say that people who are out of touch with their culture often tend to be out of touch with themselves. In fact, culture is as important to who we are as our name and social security number.

There are many cultures to which we can belong. Our family, workplace, community affiliations form the basis for a variety of cultures and subcultures that feed us and help us bring meaning to our lives. Our ethnic or historical backgrounds help to form a context of meaning as well. Our ranging tastes in the arts and yes, even pop culture, help clarify and bring us closer to who we are. It's part of the nature of humans to identify with cultural groupings; no matter how individual we fancy ourselves to be we simply cannot function, cutoff from one another. This interdependence is essential to a healthy life. We all know the expression, "we are what we eat." Likewise, we are also the cultures we embrace. As meaning making machines, we create layers of identity. Our politics, religious beliefs, values all come from the cultures with whom we identify.

So, if our culture is who we are, and if we are inextricably linked to it, then it seems to follow that it also forms the basis for what we have to offer when it comes to giving gifts. They say it is the "thought that counts" when it comes to giving and receiving gifts. Nowhere is that more true than with the gift of culture. The buying of mass-produced "stuff," and presenting it as a gift of love is, to me, the ultimate contradiction in terms.

Ironically, you will often pay much less for something that is hand-made by an artist. The most precious gift is that which expresses who we are, culturally. If ever there was a time to connect with family and friends it is now, when the hearth has taken on more significance than ever. So how can we give culture to our loved ones? Hand-made, or one-of-a-kind items reflect our culture better than any store bought item will ever do.

So here are some suggestions: how about tickets to a play, a book that moved you, an original painting or hand-blown glass vase that inspires you. Make an outing to a local gallery, museum or art center and don't forget to stop at the gift shop. Buy or make a hand-made ornament, or find a special heirloom keepsake, made in your native land. Take the time to create a photo album, or frame a picture that reminds you of a significant moment in your life. Commission an original work of art, choosing a subject, style or genre that means something to you. Compile a CD or program your ipod with your favorite music and give it to a loved one. Frame your child's artwork, the winning hockey puck, the perfect attendance certificate. Give a boutique item from an exotic, far away land. It's never too late to find deeply personal gifts that also have cultural meaning. When we give the gift of culture we give from the heart and that's what it's all about.

Secrets of the Masters Revealed

Did you ever wonder how Carvaggio was able to make his paintings seem so real or marveled at how Frans Hals could paint a laughing boy? I have. Why do you suppose so many people respond to excellent realism with, "it looks just like a photograph?" Although intended as a compliment the statement begs the question, how can representational work (created with the use of a photograph or not) transcend the level of a snapshot, where the experience of the artist is alive on the surface of the canvas?

Creating quite a stir in art circles a few years back was the book by David Hockney, *Secret Knowledge—Rediscovering the Lost Techniques of the Old Masters*. It is an exhaustive but fascinating look at the optical techniques used by the masters since about 1430 AD. Hockney postulates that even though we have proof that the giants of art used optical projections to achieve incredible detail and immediacy, in much the same way, today's artists use photography, this "Secret Knowledge" in no way diminishes their accomplishments.

Though Hockney's book demystifies the technology used by the masters it fails to truly address the dangers of relying on photography to achieve radiance and subtlety in painting. The use of such devices as the camera obscura, the camera lucida or the use of convex mirrors to create projections has been a carefully guarded secret for centuries—even today it is rarely discussed. Although the use of photography, which seems the natural evolution of these devices, is in common use today by most realists, many "purists" consider it cheating (at least publicly!).

Clearly, there is no substitute for excellent draftsmanship, the ability to see and draw without the use of aids. Hockney repeatedly points out that even with mechanical aids, it is still the artist who makes marks. No technology can make up for an untrained eye, just as no amount of state-of-the-art surgical equipment can compensate for a lack of medical training and experience.

If one accepts, after the considerable evidence presented, that many of the most beloved products of Western culture were created with the aid of mirrors and lenses then we must accept that the use of photography is the natural progression for current practitioners.

Or do we?

Cubism and post-modernism were a direct response to the advent of photography. What happened? The moment we had the ability to preserve an optical image it divided painting into two groups, the realists were suddenly wiped out like the dinosaurs, replaced with the more raw and more mannerly modernist movements. At that moment, artists who used optics were no longer compelled to be present with the subject. Realism nearly disappeared because the mystery was taken away. Now Hockney comes along and argues there wasn't really a mystery in the first place! He details how chiaroscuro, the use of strong lighting to express form, came about because of the intense light needed to create the projected image. He also includes examples of how the unique soft focus effects of paintings done with optical technologies lead to the almost "photographic" qualities present in the paintings of Vermeer and Ingres.

Although his arguments are always compelling, Hockney stops short in "Secret Knowledge" of addressing the central dilemma in the use of photography by today's realists: whether to use photography or to work from life. Many of today's top realists claim to work exclusively from life, carefully guarding their secrets, just as the old masters did. If nothing else, Hockney has revealed the in-authenticity of perpetuating this mystique. After all, if optics were good enough for Vermeer, who are we to judge?

The true mystery of painting is in the artistry of the mark made by the sure hand of talent and experience. But does working from a photograph impede or diminish our talent? Many artists find working form a photo to be limiting and frustrating. They have rejected (or at least claim to have rejected) photographic technology altogether. It's true, a photograph flattens forms and creates unnatural contrasts (take a look at Caravaggio!); shadows in photos tend to become black and we lose most of the subtlety of form and color; a camera has no ability to select what is important in an image. Yet some artists have learned to compensate, even thrive, by practicing diligently from life and applying the lessons of honest observation to photographs.

My solution has been to develop an understanding of the limits and advantages of both. When I use photography (who has time to sit for a portrait!) I bracket, getting light and dark exposures. I have studied the impact of focal length, depth of field, emulsion chemistry, lighting; in short, I have made it my business to understand the technology of photography. Even digital photography has its own limitations. Likewise I have applied myself to a careful study of values, color theory, perspective, design, anatomy and physiognomy, logging countless hours of painting and drawing from life. In other words, I have committed myself to a mastery of the technology available to me and adapted accordingly rather than buried my head in the sand. If we are not the masters of our technology we will be its slave.

True art is the difference between knowledge and experience, whether we are talking about realism or cubism. I believe realism fell out of vogue because it was caught protecting a lie. It is enjoying resurgence now because it is coming clean. This is the implied challenge of "Secret Knowledge." When talent and success are based on secrets it will almost certainly fail us. I know I am the only one who will ever paint like me, not because of technology, but because of who I am. I also know the same is true for anyone who dares to step into the arena of self-expression.

Who knows where the next Caravaggio will turn up?

Art and the Almighty Dollar

Arts people are always talking about how important the study of arts are in developing a healthy child, a vital community and a rich cultural life. But we don't always realize how important arts and culture are to our economy. Responding to a recent nationwide study entitled: Arts & Economic Prosperity: In "The economic impact of nonprofit arts organizations and their audiences," Robert Lynch, past President and CEO of Americans for the Arts stated, "when communities invest in the arts, there is a tendency to think that they are opting for cultural benefits at the expense of economic benefits. This study demonstrates that the arts are an industry that generates extraordinary economic activity, jobs, and tax revenues."

The report in question is based on surveys of 3,000 nonprofit arts organizations and 40,000 attendees at arts events in 91 cities in 33 states, plus the District of Columbia. In other words, it was pretty comprehensive.

The study found that those attending Nonprofit Arts events spend an Average of $22.87 Per Person. The impact of Nonprofit Arts Organizations translates to: Total Expenditures of $53.2 billion, 2.09 million full-time equivalent jobs, household income of $47.4 billion, Local Government Revenue of $2.4 billion, State Government Revenue of $3.0 billion, and Federal Income Tax Revenue totaling $5.6 billion. Americans for the Arts conducted the study in 91 communities back in 2000 and 2001. The diverse communities ranged in population (from 4,000 to 3,000,000), geography (Anchorage to Miami), and type (rural to large urban). The three largest U.S. cities (New York, Los Angeles, and Chicago) each with more than $1 billion in organizational expenditures alone were excluded from this study to avoid inflating the national estimates. The full text of the report is available at http://www.americansforthearts.org/EconomicImpact.

The impact of Nonprofit Arts Audiences generates total expenditures of $80.8 billion. And this was strictly in the nonprofit arts sector.

Yet, we are still under funding non-profit arts organizations. Of course, there are those among us who believe the government has no business supporting arts in the first place. What these people don't understand is that this money is a relatively small investment for a dramatic economic return, as shown above. It's not just the high profile non-profits like the Detroit Institute of Arts that would have to reduce services (along with benefits like tax revenues and jobs). We're also talking about the health of smaller grassroots arts and culture organizations, where the people live, which are the cornerstone of this economic impact. These have the most to lose with these cuts. Without the smaller, grassroots organizations like Wayne County Council for Arts, History and Humanities, The Detroit Artists Market, and others like them, the quality of life and economic viability of our community will suffer greatly.

What makes any region attractive, as a destination, is its diverse people and culture. Without adequate arts funding Michigan is looking at a very dismal future. We must stop thinking of the Arts

140

as an "elective," they are who we are! Meanwhile, artists go about the business of transforming lives, providing opportunities for full self-expression, one person at a time. The Wayne County Council for Arts, History and Humanities is working with the more than 500 arts related organizations to join in creating economically viable ARTnerships, reducing program duplication and combining resources, energy, information and experience to expand quality programming to the entire county. It's an investment in our community. It's art to believe.

Cool Cities, Warm Heart

Everyone told me, "having a baby changes everything." Now that I have two toddlers I begin to discover the truth in that statement. Resisting the impulse to gush about the miracle of childhood I can safely say that my children have significantly changed my perspective. For one thing, I now know first-hand, spit happens. From a broader perspective, I'm finding myself much more deeply concerned about where our world is heading.

Consequently, I am even more committed to identifying what it means to be human in a society gone mad. Sure I can provide Danny and Mary a stimulating home life and engage them creatively. I can let them know they are part of an amazing array of diverse cultures and possibilities. But what happens when they discover the intolerance, greed and insensitivity of the world outside our home? What can I do to improve their chances of growing up in a humane society? I can't help but ponder what the ultimate purpose of our government should be in this effort. Is it to provide moral guidance, legislating right from wrong? Or is it simply to provide services and opportunities, leaving moral choices to the individual? Once, it was the artists, teachers and religious leaders who vied for the hearts and minds of the individual, not the politicians. I wonder whatever happened to the politicians who stood for getting government off our backs? There is a growing, moral arrogance in our government and it's very frightening.

POINT OF ART

Our second President, John Adams, once said, and I'm paraphrasing, "I became a warrior and a politician so my children could become scientists and teachers, so their children could become artists and poets." A great many people have made it possible for us to enjoy the benefits of a civilized world, no more so than our soldiers who have fought and died for your freedom.

Yet, judging from our behavior as a society, we are not learning the lessons of our own history. We have marginalized the arts, history and humanities to the point of insignificance, rather than looking to the creative class to show the way. In an elusive quest for high test scores we are turning our classrooms into an obedience training circus, producing trained seals, instead of well-rounded human beings. These are fairly modern phenomenon; at one time artists and teachers were indeed not just the mirrors of society but the very framework itself. From ancient Greece, through the Medici to Roosevelt's Public Works of Art, artists have always been called upon to get the economic ball rolling. SOHO, in New York City is a more modern example of the powerful transformation artists can ignite.

Fortunately there are hopeful signs that the pendulum is finally beginning to swing back; artists are once again being encouraged to play a powerful role in the re-building of our communities.

There has been much talk over the years about the "Cool Cities" initiative. If you have not gotten hip to this movement, here's your chance to do so. The stakes have never been higher. "Those regions that do not flourish in the new creative economy will fail," according to Carnegie Mellon University professor Richard Florida, author of "The Rise of the Creative Class." His theories about urban planning and his identification of the Creative Class as the key to economic development are gaining credibility.

Florida's groundbreaking book is heralding a new age of economic-development for several major metropolitan areas, hopefully to a community near you.

Its basic theory suggests that a strong creative community leads to a better family life. I like to think of it as an investment in my children's future.

Please, No More
Starving Artists

If I never hear the expression, "starving artist" again it won't be soon enough for me. The old scarcity paradigm that says there is only so much wealth, recognition, talent, etc. to go around, is due for a serious overhaul. The idea that the world is a big pie with only so many slices still seems to dominate the thinking of our arts community. The question is this: are full self-expression and financial success really mutually exclusive?

I'm sick of the people who believe that if an artist is able to sell his/her work then they are commercial sell-outs. There is no more market driven vocation in the world than that of a fine artist.

Let's start with the most basic reason artists create in the first place—to express their unique experience of humanity. The question is why? Or more to the point, why bother? The answer is that we must. But why must we express? The reason is that in any society there are a few among us who feel the need to connect their experience of the world with others. I don't buy it when an artist says he has culled his most precious ideas into being, only to please himself. The fact is, artists must effectively communicate their ideas to others if they are to survive as professionals.

I may be overly dependent on what people think of me—and believe me, I have received considerable therapy on this issue—but I don't see the point of getting out of bed, if not to make some kind of an impact on, and be impacted by, other human beings. So if we accept that artists are those who have found a way to effectively express themselves to others, then we must also accept that professional artists are subject to the same economics inherent in all human interaction. No man is an island. The arts community has devised many ways to insulate itself from the free market. Some seek the security of academia, where tenured professors are paid by idealistic students to teach them not to expect to make a living as an artist for fear of corrupting the purity of their expression. Easy for them, they have a job!

Another insulating institution is the non-profit system, which makes government or private funding available to artists pursuing ostensibly "non-commercial" projects. I'm not saying for a minute that academia or the non-profit sector is not enormously important in our society. The point is that in whatever system we choose to operate—whether academia, non-profit, commercial art or working with a gallery—professional artists must play the game of obtaining recognition, grants, commissions, awards and yes, sales.

It is our failure to communicate the importance of the arts in our society that keeps artists "starving." It astounds me when artists themselves romanticize the notion of the "starving artist." If we don't begin to reverse our own attitudes that art is not really an essential part of the human experience then we are destined to remain on the short end of the economic stick. We artists need to value—and educate others to value—our creativity if we want to thrive. Creative people must stop short-selling their God-given talents. That means reaching out to others and commanding respect. We must get into the arena and master the game if we are going to call ourselves professionals. Get that PhD, learn to write an award-winning grant, knock the socks off an art gallery, hone your creative voice and master your craft. But first be an artist who needs people (cue the music!).

It's easy to give our talent away and gripe about how little money there is for the arts. But let's not kid ourselves; that's not being an artist. The challenges facing professional artists take every fiber of our being to overcome. The truth is there is no such thing as a starving artist. Professional artists don't starve or have "day jobs"—plain and simple. The world is brimming with unlimited abundance if we are willing to figure out and do what it takes to connect with it. We must adjust our expectations to fit our vision of what the world has to offer. If we believe in a world where art isn't important then we have no right to expect anything from it. Being a professional artist is a lifetime adventure of commitment that takes talent, drive, vision—and plenty to eat!

Art Takes a Community— Investing in Our Stakeholders

After 9-11 we all were forced to take a deeper look at our lives and what was important to us. As an active member of Detroit's arts community I found myself taking a hard look at how each of us defines success. One art dealer/artist from Windsor once described Detroit as the "wild wild west of the art world."

"Anything goes" is the first and only rule. I imagine Detroit is not unique in this chaotic soup of mavericks fighting to promote themselves in a competitive world. In Detroit's market driven mind-set one might assume that what floats to the top is the cream. Unfortunately, that's not always the case.

What are the main criteria for success in the art community? Is it money, as in most other businesses? Is market driven art somehow better art? I've talked with many who believe the answer to both questions is "yes." But there is a lot of schlock that commands a large percentage of the profits in the huge commercial fine art industry. So-called "starving artist" art, made anonymously in a factory, is sold at wholesale for the cost of a bad haircut. It is the then marked up as much as a hundred times the original price by commercial galleries and decorators. By any standard of quality, appealing to the lowest common denominator does not make for the most "successful" art. On the other hand, many established contemporary artists sell their work for thousands or even millions of dollars. But does a high price tag necessarily mean the art is better? Is money really the only criteria for success? Of course not.

So how do we define success in the art world? To answer that question we have to take a look at how successfully our arts organizations and artists are serving the various stakeholders in their community. The hallmarks of success vary widely, depending on whether we're talking about galleries, art dealers, art brokers, art consultants, appraisers, museums, educational institutions, nonprofit art centers, service organizations or the artists themselves. In a healthy arts community, each of these entities works in tandem to serve the various stakeholders that make up the community as a whole (by the way, if you have read this far, you are hereby an official member of the arts community!).

I have noticed that these distinctions are a little blurry in Detroit's arts community. Many organizations (even artists) want to be all things to all people. While on the surface this sounds like a good idea I have found it often leads to confusion and diffusion of services. What many people don't realize is that each of these entities has an implied primary constituency. Firemen put out fires and protect the public. The public is their primary stakeholder. Stockbrokers trade stocks to the advantage of their clients (well, at least they're supposed to!). A Doctor's primary stakeholder is his or her patients.

Likewise, in the arts community, the non-profit art guilds/ clubs serve their member artists. They exist to showcase, educate and promote their members. When these organizations try to become art dealers on behalf of their member-artists a conflict naturally arises, as the art buyer then becomes their primary stakeholder. Having art for sale may be one way a guild or club can promote their artists. But when the art buyer then becomes their stakeholder then the organization has changed its purpose and should change its mission accordingly.

A non-profit museum or art center, such as the Detroit Institute of Art, serves primarily to educate and enlighten the public. They are not answerable to the artist or the art buyer, though they may serve them. They depend on public funding to operate, such as grants, ticket sales, contributions and endowments.

By definition, the art dealer, consultant and gallery serve the collector. In the process of serving the buyer the art dealer serves the artist, who benefits from the sale of his/her work. The art dealer's primary stakeholder must be the buyer. If an art dealer attempted to operate as a museum or an art guild, without the benefit of public funding (or personal wealth) to support the operation, it would be a recipe for failure, serving no one. Sadly, this is often the case. Fortunately (or unfortunately) we have a number of vanity galleries, which are insulated from the market by personal wealth.

Who is the primary stakeholder of the fine artist? Are they their own constituency, as many fine artists believe? Or are their stakeholders their past and future buyers? If so, what are the ways in which the fine artist reaches these buyers? Fine artists promote themselves in a number of ways: they exhibit, compete for awards, apply for grants. They may occasionally sell through art guilds, art fairs, even restaurants. Some artists create their own unique opportunities for exhibition and publicity. Some fine artists promote/support themselves through teaching while others have "day jobs." To be "successful," however, fine artists hire brokers/agents or work directly through an art dealer, whose job it is to serve his/her buyers, which in turn, serves the artist.

Many artists misunderstand this relationship. Rather than treating them as partners they resent the art dealers and begrudge the crucial role they play in the community.

In addition, many art dealers have turned their backs on artists in response to this resentment. Unfortunately, that's one reason there are so few contemporary galleries specializing in local talent. I have noticed two things that distinguish successful art markets like Chicago, Santa Fe and Ashville: 1) The value of artwork is higher and more consistent and 2) there is a strong sense of gallery loyalty on the part of artists. Consequently, in these centers, collectors know where to find the artists work and how such it will cost. Detroit's fine artists' misguided practice of showing their work wherever and whenever possible, essentially flooding the market, is driving the value of everyone's work down the tubes.

I'm sick of hearing about how there's no demand or appreciation for contemporary art in this town. Trust me, there's a huge untapped market for serious contemporary art in metro Detroit, as there is in most economic centers.

Let's just say it's currently a buyer's market (which on the surface would seem to be great news to fledgling collectors). Our artists and art dealers need to wake up and begin working for the greater good if they ever want to be taken seriously by the thousands of potential art collectors who don't as yet know we exist.

Now is the time to take action in our community. There is a critical need for unity and clarification as the many arts organizations and artists compete for funding and support from their respective constituents during this economic slow-down. On the bright side, there are a number of excellent models within our community. The Detroit Institute of Arts is doing a fantastic job of

ROBERT MANISCALCO

identifying and appealing to their stakeholders—the general public. Smaller non-profits, like the Detroit Artists Market and the Grosse Pointe Artists Association, are thriving as they focus on their stakeholders—their members. There are a few contemporary commercial galleries/dealers, who are very quietly identifying their stakeholders (the collectors) and moving local art into people's homes and businesses while others are scrambling to please other artsits.

Fortunately, I work with a great many artists and others in our community who are committed to creating a viable Detroit art market. Likewise, artists and the organizations that serve them need to organize and build on successful models from other communities.

It comes down to each of us taking personal responsibility to reach out and to educate. Collectors need to be taught to tell their friends about their latest acquisition. Artists also need to be taught how to participate in the effective promotion of their work. I believe together, we can serve the best interests of the entire community, making it an even more compelling and exciting place to live and raise our families. After all, that's what success is all about.

Art Education and World Peace

We all know that an arts education is an integral part of becoming a professional artist. It is also integral to becoming a fully functional human being. The arts have a way of opening up and developing the whole person. In school, we are taught how to survive. We learn that red means stop, and green means give it the gas. We are taught our right hand from our left, that grass is green, that the sky is blue, night time is dark, etc. While this kind of education may serve to help children make sense of the awesome world around them, it is not the whole picture. And yet as we grow into adults we are asked to continue this neat segregation into categories. We are taught, for instance, that the color black is evil and that white is holy, which eventually translates to read, "black people are to be feared and white people are the good guys." Then, when we are all grown up, we are taught that Walmart is evil and Republicans are good—no wait a minute, that was last year! In other words, we are taught to add meaning to things around us in order to create agreement. Without consensus, the reasoning goes, we will cease to function as a society. We seem to be saying, "if you agree with me, no one will get hurt!"

The point is that we have been taught to stereotype and make ever-broadening generalizations about the world. It is part of the very fabric of our educational system. Not that schools teach racism or xenophobia. It is the nature of our black and white education that leads us to become racist. In this context it is not hard to understand why our society suffers from the scourge of racism and our world is racked by nationalism and religious extremism. Have you ever wondered why the Israelis and the Palestinians refuse to get along? They've been carefully taught not to. It is not because the children of Iran lack education in the three "R's" that allows religious zealots to rise to power, it is the disconnect with their own culture and the restrictions of their creative freedoms that drive down their society.

By exercising the right-brain, which gives us the ability to see in the abstract perception of line, form, color, as well as complex political and social concepts, we begin to view the world objectively, rather than subjectively. We begin to see in shades of gray rather than black and white. To express a line of music or dance we begin to experience our senses in a profound, universal ecstasy. It reaches into our soul in a way reading *Time Magazine* can't. Self-expression is visceral. When fully self-expressed the soul experiences a one-ness with the universe—an inner peace that makes us more sensitive, present, in short, more human.

There is no right and wrong in art, no moral imperative. Developing artistic skills requires discipline, focus and inner freedom. Artistic accomplishment creates self-esteem and provides an access to our higher power—a connection, one to another.

It is important that we consider the possibility that public education caters almost exclusively to the left-brain. As the arts have been dropped from the curriculum and schools have concentrated more and more on achieving higher test scores to satisfy federal mandates our society is losing its ability to function in a humane way. I am so grateful I had art and music when I was growing up. As I present workshops in the inner city I see the children who have never been exposed to the arts. There is a deadness in their eyes that makes me sad in my heart.

The arts have a way of bringing the right-side of the brain into the process of solving problems. The arts have a way of breaking the cycle of mendacity and desperation that poisons our communities.

Most artists have developed the ability to create opportunities where there didn't seem to be any. This is the true meaning of creativity and it is probably the single most important survival skill an individual can learn. The goal of any arts education or arts mentoring program is to provide an opportunity for students to discover alternative methods of survival and expand their ability to cope with the challenges facing them every day with creativity and trust. That is the powerful potential of a good arts education.

Am I saying the arts are the key to world peace? Indeed I am! Help stamp out cultural illiteracy and war. Sign your child up for ballet today.

Pop Culture Alert

We are constantly barraged with the empty promises of popular culture (the other PC!). It seems everywhere we turn people are trying to get us to buy something. Commerce is, after all, the driving force behind pop culture. We are programmed to crave the familiar. We go to McDonalds to be taken care of by Ronald. We surf the radio, the TV, the web, looking for something, anything. We let them fill our tired minds with the dribble that keeps us plugged in and tuned out. Have you ever turned off the TV in the middle of an important talk show discussing an evocative issue, say teen boys sleeping with their girlfriend's mother, only to forget the topic moments after? It's because popular culture is merely topical medication—it doesn't treat the cause, only the symptoms of our longing for true inspiration and meaning.

We long to be moved in a life changing way—to be truly transported, not just distracted. Pop culture plays on that need but can never satisfy it. That's something only the arts can do for us. I'm speaking of a great film that rises above the Hollywood ending, an original painting, where you can feel the presence of the artist in his brush strokes, a piece of music with structure and color that challenges the senses, a play that teaches and surprises us. These are the stuff of catharsis. These stay with us even after they are gone. Art is what teaches us to be human. We live in a world that confuses art with entertainment. There are significant differences, however. Art is an active process. Entertainment only pacifies us. Art has power in it. Entertainment is powerful only in it's ability to compel the masses. Pop culture markets individuality (i.e. Nike), art expresses it. Individuality is not only expressed by the creator but by the individual who is moved to action by the creation. The statement, "this is art," is not only an expression of our taste but a statement of who we are as individuals.

In the hands of a great artist mass mediums such as film and popular music have occasionally risen to high levels of both art and entertainment. Of course, any such assessments are purely subjective. But isn't our opinion, ultimately, the only means of expressing our individuality? Sadly, most people can't or are unwilling to distinguish between art and mere entertainment. It is a laziness that has been programmed into us over years of a mass bombardment by pop culture. We say, true creative epiphanies are too much bother, take too much time or are too far over our heads. Nothing is further from the truth. You don't have to be smart or rich to be inspired. Art is like eating, sleeping or a warm embrace. All we have to do is raise the food to our lips, fall onto our pillows or slide into the arms of our lover. As we allow ourselves to enter deeper into the creative process, gently encouraging our senses, it becomes ever more satisfying. The difference between McDonalds and, say, Commanders Palace is worth the time, money and energy it takes to experience true culinary ecstasy.

Sensitivity to beauty, a deeper cultural awareness, doesn't come with wealth or conventional education. Granite counter tops or BMWs are no substitute for a work of art or a performance that deeply moves, touches and inspires us.

Of course so much art falls short of inspiration that we've grown cynical. Art has become elitist. In this world of over stimulation it's difficult to hear the still voice of inspiration. But we can hear it if we listen. It's there in the tapping foot of an elementary school band student, lost in the reverie of his first spring concert, the first painting done by a man in his sixties.

On the other hand, labeling something as "high art" in no way guarantees a life changing catharsis, which is the lofty intention of full self expression. I'm talking about art that lays bare the vulnerable soul of the creator. Being disappointed is the chance we take as we venture forth into the world of truth and beauty.

How dull our lives would be without those occasional moments of revelation and ecstasy. We must hold forth, however frustrating the journey. This all may seem obvious to fellow art spirits; if you've read this far you probably already know what I'm talking about. On the other hand, each of us needs to take responsibility for gently leading the way. Not by preaching (like I'm doing now!), but in small ways—by taking action. We all can engage in little acts of daring, like telling a great story to friends, getting down on the floor and painting with children or taking a stand on censorship. Go to a concert. Take in an exhibit at a local art gallery (the best free show in town) or museum. Draw a picture on a birthday card. Turn off the TV. See a play. Doodle. Write a poem. Make up a song as you go. Don't apologize for singing out loud, or sharing your unique view on a touchy issue. Go ahead. Make my metaphor!

When will we stop thinking of fine art, music, dance, theatre and literature as expendable luxuries or non-essential highbrow fluff for other people to appreciate? As we look across the dinner table, at our family, let us give pause to what it is that makes life worth living. Its meaningful relationships with our family, our friends and the people in our lives. We all want to be close to the people that matter in our life. There are no instructions for being human. But we do have art to light the way. The arts are the closest thing we have to instructions for being alive; it is what makes each of us truly human. It's what brings people together.

What Should Artists Do with Their Unsold Artwork?

Should artists warehouse their unsold artwork or gift if out to friends and family? That's an important question for all artists to ask. The first thing that comes to my mind is the image, back in the 1970's, when my father led a protest in Detroit. Artworks were burned and/or ripped to shreds because of a conflict between the laws governing the inheritance tax and fair market value. He had tried to deduct the fair market value of an artwork when he donated it to charity. He was audited by the IRS and eventually lost his case in the U.S. Court of Appeals Tax Court.

He lost because of a law past by Congress in response to Nixon's attempt to donate his papers to his library at an exorbitant fair market value ($400,000). As a result of this law, if an artist donates an artwork to charity or to a museum they can only deduct the cost of materials. Meanwhile, many artists are causing a financial burden to their heirs when they leave an estate with lots of unsold artworks; the heirs are taxed based on the fair market value.

There's a bill that's been floating around congress for years that would remedy this inequity.

POINT OF ART

Having said all that, what is really going on behind the artist's decision to warehouse works of art? There are several root issues. Artists fail to find markets for their work because they're too lazy or too intimated about approaching galleries or alternative spaces. Ultimately, you should be thinking of establishing gallery relationships in several cities, depending on how prolific you are.

Approaching galleries has to be done in person where professional relationships can be built over time. Determine if there is a need for your work by visiting the gallery before there is any solicitation on your part. It's called market research. Once you've found a fit, I recommend you make yourself invaluable to the gallery by volunteering to help out at openings, etc. This tends to open them up to considering your work. Here are a few more dos and don'ts for winning the hearts of gallery directors: never waste a gallery director's time with idle chat. Don't describe your work over the phone. Don't monopolize their time during openings. If you are lucky enough to be accepted in a gallery be sure to keep a consistent retail value. Consider yourself part of the sales team—bring in some of the business. Share your local list with the gallery. Spend some time at the gallery that is showing your work—add value to the product. Of course, some people prefer to skip the middleman and sell at art fairs.

Warehousing artworks, out of public view, keeping them off the market is a smart thing to do if the work is not up to the high standards you've worked so hard to establish. Another good reason for warehousing is if you are in the process of building a body of work for a show.

Most amateur or student artists who paint whatever they feel like, an abstract today, an impressionist painting tomorrow, collect a lot of works that do not have any relationship to one another. There may be one or two among them that are the beginnings of a body of work worthy of exhibition but they never follow through with the series. This hit or miss approach results in a lot of work hanging around the house. As of this writing, I'm working on a series of South Carolina Lowcountry paintings— works incorporating the Gullah people that are specific to my particular geographic and cultural region in SC. It's a very specific theme and it takes a lot of focus from me to spin fresh ideas day in and day out. But since I've found a market for such work I'm motivated to continue to explore the possibilities and produce more work.

But what about those experimental, often very worthwhile artworks you don't quite know what to do with? Should we keep them at home or give/lend them to friends and family? I know an artist who lends art to people for whom he cares and who are smitten by a particular work of his, with the agreement that they can never sell it. It is theirs on permanent loan. He asks that they return it once they are no longer exhibiting it in their home. Nor is it to be transferred to their heirs once they've died. This same artist also makes a point not to sell certain major works to individuals, holding out for public collections, even if it means getting less money.

I keep straying from the question at hand because it keeps evoking deeper questions. Okay, here's my best answer to the original question about whether to give your work away. One should rarely give artwork away. Personally, it's against my religion. My goal is to stamp out the notion of the starving artist.

There are so many alternatives to giving it away. My best friend is a major collector of my work and he's gotten very good deals on the purchase of my work because he does it often, buying 2-3 paintings at a time. He also is very creative about bartering for things I need. I once gave him a small painting in exchange for a king size bed he had in storage. Bartering is much easier with family and friends. I've given discounts to people for throwing a party celebrating their new acquisition, letting me use it for exhibition or paying me in cash. What I don't do is give a discount for nothing. On the other hand, giving or lending art to loved ones or fans of your work can be an excellent piece of marketing if you know they will have a certain amount of foot traffic in their homes, i.e. parties, etc., resulting in good word-of-mouth PR for you. There is some value in that. Let's face it, even in the extreme case of giving (or deeply discounting) a work of art out of love implies getting something in return: more love. Love is always the exception.

Is There Truth in Beauty?

Anything that's complicated desires to be simplified. Anything that's simple wants to be specific. Anything that's specific brings us closer to the truth. The way to find the truth in our work is to find that which is imperfect and celebrate it's specificity. People often confuse the universal with the general. I'm not talking about details when I say "be specific." Being specific about the large important masses will get us closer to the subject's essential truth than any amount of superficial details our ego "sees." The amount of finish or detail in your work is an entirely subject choice and not subject to my opinion, or yours for that matter. Leave that to the critics.

As artists we care about getting the important things true; by true I mean rich and essential. There is always time for that which is important. Something that is important to me may not be important to you. But there are a number of concrete truths about the way a viewer connects to our work. To know these, and control them is the path to being a successful artist. I know about 50 things that are true about painting realism which are not subjective. They are not techniques; they are methods that have stuctures. I'm here to help you see better, not necessarily paint better (although that is a likely outcome). Here's one: "no two shapes in nature are exactly alike." Our job as realists is to be able to see nature as God created it, not how we think it is. What happens along that path is called art, whether we think it is good art or not, is not our concern.

My job as teacher is to demystify the process of painting, which to some may like ruining the card trick. But who would you rather be, the audience or the Magician? We must take off the "critic" hat and see what is really there in front of us. In the time it takes to eat an egg I can teach how to be a chicken. It's like riding a horse. You want it to go where you want it to go but you also want an exciting ride. Perfection is not the standard, even if it may be a goal. If I can help you get on the horse and ride or lay an egg, then I have succeeded as a teacher, even if you are a farm animal.

My Love / Hate
Relationship With Form

I *feel* I am an exceptionally handsome man trapped in an average looking man's body, which can be pretty frustrating. And I know I'm not alone. It's deeply human that I should "trouble deaf heaven with my bootless cries . . . wishing me like to one more rich in hope, featured like him, like him with friends possessed." The trouble is, this quest for more or better than what is ("desiring this man's art, and that man's scope") results in more and more misery. How do we reverse this destructive paradigm? De-emphasizing physical form is a good start; choosing not to buy into all the hype about youth and beauty helps. Of course, we all know how difficult this is when we are bombarded with images of desire every minute. My answer has been to tune out and tune in whenever I have a choice.

Also, knowing if someone walks by me because I don't fit their image of ideal physical beauty, or their idea of a talented, smart, charming or righteous person, that THEY are suffering more than I. I now feel only compassion for them, because I truly have come to hate that anybody should suffer. Now that I no longer "suffer fools," (I don't really think they're fools!) they no longer effect me -- much! The focus of my attention is reserved for those who accept me for who I am, different though I may seem, from them. I am finding these differences, more often than not, are merely an illusion created by ego, our meaning-making machine. I learn what I can from the critics and move on. And guess what; this detachment from form allows me to see it more clearly as an artist. Nice bonus!

More and more of us are becoming aware that a preoccupation with form is inextricably linked with human suffering even as we are constantly bombarded by it. I find it amazing that just looking in the mirror can trigger a desire to be more than I am; but of course the beautiful image I have of myself will never be found in the mirror. It cannot be seen by anyone, except maybe my dog, who loves me "unconditionally" because I created a *condition* whereby, in a state of unawareness, I callously replaced his mother with me, thinking he wouldn't notice. I must remind myself that the "it" that I *am* is not my visage (real or wished for), my talents, not even my thoughts.

At my most blissful, I am the Seer, watching this ego dance and marveling at the folly of it all. And this Seer is one with a Universal Source of energy, together with other Seers, who have no beginning and no end. This energy has no meaning, the ever present companion of form, at least that we will ever *know* absolutely, trapped in "this mortal coil." The only answer is to die. Not necessarily in the inevitably physical sense, but most certainly in the spiritual sense. I must accept that I am that I am only in this moment.

If a belief in God helps me accomplish that, then great. If I choose to imbue "Him" with the form of an old man with white robes, more power to me. But understanding that none of us can ever know for certain beyond the limits of this form, I now find myself free of the trappings of form. I see beauty without judgment. For me, any experience of religion can only come out of my being firmly established in this most basic spiritual practice of acceptance. I chose the form in which I am contained and the gift of life I'm living because it's available to me now. And that gives me great pleasure. I can say with all honesty I accept you. This moment is mine for an unknowable period of time, on loan from the vast library of the Universe. It may not be tomorrow. The here and now is all I truly have. My dog knows this well; that's why he's so happy, even without his mother.

The Competitive Edge

It's very simple: if we want to win more awards, commissions, fellowships, accolades (has anyone ever seen an accolade?), we all know we must make exceptional art. But to make exceptional art we have to clearly understand the structures we employ and execute our work within our chosen framework. In order to execute our structures we have to practice the fundamental elements required to succeed within that framework.

That means practicing and learning, backwards and forwards, what is required of us at every moment during the process. For instance, if you employ figuration in your work, it may help to spend time in sketch class. To be able to accomplish that we need a mastery of the basic visual elements, which in the case of painting represenationally, involve value, edges, draftsmanship, texture, etc.

Assimilating these require focused repetition, which means showing up (half the battle), being 100% PRESENT, body and soul. It means studying those who are/were successful doing what you want to be doing. Remember, in these high level disciplines we are really playing against ourselves, that part of us that doesn't really have the time to do what it might take with everything else that's pulling on us: the kids, the jobs, the spouse, the TV (really, the TV?).

ROBERT MANISCALCO

This is the truth of it. It's easy to be a success when we know what we're doing and we have something important to say and everyone thinks we're wonderful and values our time. It's not as easy when other artists seem to be getting ahead, making it look so easy when perhaps they may have dedicated their lives to mastering their respective structures.

With people like them wondering the planet why would anyone really care about your art? Even though we know these are external factors beyond our control, they gnaw at our ego, and we get tired and feel defeated. Success gives us extra super powers called confidence. But it also gives the other guy confidence when we perceive them as having it all together. That's why we must discipline ourselves not to care about how well the other guy is doing. Sometimes, in that moment when another artist "wins" we just want to run away and hide. Giving in to that feeling only gives the other guy more power over you, for which I can assure you, he has absolutely no use.

So it is in those moments we have to understand it has very little to do with the other guy and everything to do with what we are doing. If they win, good for them. "Now it's my turn," then becomes our mantra. That's when it really gets to be about winning that battle within ourselves and committing to doing what we've practiced. It is the inner game of art. If we give away our confidence, lose heart, and we're not in all the way, can we really expect to get ahead in this or any other realm? We must dedicate ourselves to the game we have chosen to play, the one we have practiced, even when we didn't want to.

We have all experienced the bitter pill of losing, even though we felt certain we had the raw talent to succeed. We may even feel entitled. But all the bravado and false confidence in the world won't make you a success. It may for a while, but it won't last. Raw,

170

unfocussed talent will never be enough to move the ball down the field. It's going to take commitment and focus to make our art, which in turn will lead to confidence, no matter what the external conditions. Repetition is the only path to success. There is no substitute for being prepared.

The Artist as a Lifestyle Entrepreneur

People often think of the life of an artist as an entrepreneurial endeavor. But let's be specific. According to Wikipedia professional artists are considered "Lifestyle Entrepreneurs" because we "place passion before profit when launching a business in order to combine personal interests and talent with the ability to earn a living." The pure definition of an entrepreneur are those primarily motivated by the intention to make their business profitable in order to sell it to shareholders. That's not us. "In contrast, a lifestyle entrepreneur intentionally chooses a business model intended to develop and grow their business in order to make a long-term, sustainable and viable living working in a field where they have a particular interest, passion, talent, knowledge or high degree of expertise.

A lifestyle entrepreneur may decide to become self-employed in order to achieve greater personal freedom, more family time and more time working on projects or business goals that inspire them. A lifestyle entrepreneur may combine a hobby with a profession or they may specifically decide not to expand their business in order to remain in control of their venture. Common goals held by the lifestyle entrepreneur include earning a living doing something that they love, earning a living in a way that facilitates self-employment, achieving a good work/life balance and owning a business without

POINT OF ART

Shareholders, where a passion before profit approach to entrepreneurship often prevails. While many entrepreneurs may launch their business with a clear exit strategy, a lifestyle entrepreneur may deliberately and consciously choose to keep their venture fully within their own control."

As artists we have a calling. We have something unique to say. The age old question is how much, if at all, we should/must adapt our vision to suit the market? Or rather should we not just redouble our efforts toward finding and/or creating a market for our vision? While the later may be the road less traveled it ultimately contains the deeper reward. Typically, it comes down to whether you would rather be "right" or "happy?"

My question is do you have what it takes to create a healthy balance between these conflicting states of being? Here's the equation: right + happy = success. The key is to accept the seemingly impossible challenges in remaining "pure" and honoring your vision. In other words are you willing to find the bliss in the process, which will include finding/generating your niche market, wherever that may lead you?

The alternative is that you may find yourself in the miserable position of adapting your vision to your IDEA of the market. I know many people who have sold out their integrity and never gotten paid a dime for doing it. I see talented artists (actors, dancers, writers, composers, fill in the blank) painting to their warped idea of what they think will sell, only to be surprised and disillusioned when they fail.

Art is a calling, a lifestyle. You must choose to either listen to the call and attack the challenge of marketing with joy or be prepared to go out and get a real job. Suffering for your art need not be integral to the process. It's simply not a sustainable model.

The Key to Success

I am often asked what is the secret to being a successful artist. In these missives I have been attempting to get at that question from a variety of angles. As always I encourage readers to go back and read past emails or get a copy of my book for some concrete, as well as philosophical answers to that question. Success takes on many forms: longevity in the business, intrinsic quality of the work itself, income derived from the activity. But for me, at this point, it is primarily about my own level of satisfaction with the entire process. Because I know if I'm enjoying the process, moment by moment, all the other elements are much more likely to fall into place.

I have now been painting portraits for about 31 years. It has been an amazing arch filled with rich stories, deep personal connections to others and profound self-discovery. I can tell you the reason I have lasted so long is because I understood from the beginning the importance of giving up my ego, to tap into a deeper fountain of past and present knowledge and inspiration. It has never been about me but rather my connection with the Source of all knowledge and wisdom. This has given my work an authority that could not have happened in the vacuum of "finding myself." It has produced a high level of consistency that is essential in any profession. I think about a baseball player batting with a .450 average and imagine the dismal failure I would be with such an average! To be successful in my business you have to bat 1,000. One or two homeruns just won't cut it. That's why I have so many paintings on my website, rather than the recommended 3-4 samples. So to those just beginning their careers I encourage you to make a lifetime commitment to study and building and growing throughout the years. I can tell you with certainty, none of us will ever "arrive" until we die so you may as well enjoy the process of becoming.

How Much for that Cool Painting?

I am often asked this question by those who may still associate having their portrait painted with possessing an over-sized ego. First, because you are my email friend and in consideration of how our lives have been drawn together, I want to give you a thoughtful answer and not some stock marketing verbiage: because there is something fascinating and appealling about virtually everyone, including you.

You may never have considered having a portrait painted. My intention is not to convince you that you or someone you love and admire is indeed worthy of a portrait. Our egos tend to point us to an assessment of your accomplishments, your position, the perception of your form, the influence you have in society, in short, the -ness of you. None of these things are sufficient reasons to pay my ridiculous fee. After all, the person I am painting is really none of those things. I have first hand experience that underneath all the stuff we associate with you there is a very special person that is one with all the universe. It is that person, the seer of your thoughts, that I am interested in painting.

The first thing my son Danny printed on his new label maker he got for his birthday was, "I love everyone and everything." Because I agree with Danny, I realize there is truly something intrinsically lovable in everyone and everything.

POINT OF ART

I have come to know that you, because you are a one-up manifestation of God, are worthy of a great portrait. I see and want to express that glimmer in your eye. That part of you that doesn't quit. The part that longs for a better world but celebrates the world we have with every part of your being. I think too there is an inherent curiosity about how a great artist perceives us.

I believe portraiture is a powerful tool that teaches us all how to love and appreciate our fellow beings, human or other. In fact, it's not about us, not even that seer-of-our-thoughts, one-with-the-universe essence. It is always about others and our connections with their essences. I paint people and other beings because they inspire me. That is why I have dedicated the last 31 years, my entire adult life, to painting portraits, and not just landscapes. It's not for the money (though I certainly do appreciate it!) or the thrill of fighting, and sometimes losing out to, my competition.

I do it because it is important that a permanant record be made of our precious time on this Earth. I've come to appreciate the way a great oil-on-canvas portrait expresses the quintessential personality, character and soul of the subject, capturing it for the ages. An oil portrait or drawing says so much more than a mere photograph and adds weight, warmth and humanity to the life of all who see it.

I call my style "expressive realism," because I allow the paint to tell much of the story, rather than being too heavy handed and making it look like a photograph. You might also notice a distinct feeling of light that sets it apart from other artists working today. The reason I've stayed in business all this time is because I enjoy looking deeply at the inside. Honest observation, an almost journalistic love affair with the study of humanity and what makes us tick. Whenever possible, I enjoy a collaboration with my sitters so I can really understand their vision for the finished work. It's all part of my mission to celebrate my connection with others. For we mustn't forget we are never alone.

Transformations

One of my students just shared this with me, which left me feeling deeply grateful and humble. It also got me thinking:

"I haven't told you, but you are such a good art teacher. I have improved so much with your help, and feel like the sky is the limit. Painting has given me a life again, after 15 years without one. Being in pain and trying to live with it was all I knew - now I feel as if I have another chance at a happy and productive life. Thanks so much!"

I have noticed the absence of pain when I paint (or teach or act or write), among other wonderful benefits when deeply engrossed in the creative process. I have always been a staunch believer in the transformative powers of being IN the creative process. People often tell me how time seems to pass so quickly when painting, etc. Why is this? I think when humans take the focus off themselves, give their ego a rest, we are literally transported to another spiritual plane. The deeper our study, our inquiry, the deeper our concentration, the more amazing this time travel phenomenon becomes. It actually lessons physical (and emotional) pain, because it takes our focus completely outside of ourselves. With a little structured focus it can become almost an out of body experience, requiring no drugs or outside stimulation at all (see "The Case for Painting Sober" below). I have equated it to my yoga experience in the past because the creative process is most definitely a yoga experience; it is a profound meditation. I have constructed exercises to gain immediate access to this plane, heavily borrowed from the thousands of teachers who came before me, over thousands of years. I believe the arts are the key to peace on Earth, beginning with peace in me. I explored this a bit in the Van Gogh play, among other ideas.

The Case for Painting Sober

Have you noticed the rise of all the Bottles and Brush type businesses, offering a fun, easy painting experience over a glass or two or three of wine? These places are literally overflowing with drunken, brush wielding Van Gogh wannabees having great fun. What once was the sacred realm of the talented elite has now been democratized, resulting in self expression for all, which BTW, is something I have always supported. After all, why should all the creative fun be in the hands of the 1% who are "serious" about their art?

One of my goals has always been to take the pressure of genius out of the equation of self expression. For the last thirty years, I believed I had found a sure-fire way to guarantee success by simplifying and quantifying the methods of the masters. I called this process "The Power of Positive Painting," the premise being that if you learned a few basic concepts about value and observational drawing you could then become the master of your own creativity and along the way, find your unique voice as an artist. Talent be damned! I defined art as that amazing thing that happens while we are focusing on a simple structure. In fact I wrote a book, called Point of Art, about how self-expression is not only healthy for the soul, but an inalienable right for all people.

For years I was known as the guy who could turn anyone with an open mind and a willingness to put out a little effort into a successful artist. I've coaxed photo realists and abstract expressionists into being, focusing on teaching only simple, concrete elements, never imposing my style or tastes on anyone. I'm proud to say I've trained quite a number of professional artists, with whom many I now compete (I really should be holding back some of my best secrets, but I just can't myself!). I have also opened many doors for people who didn't believe they could ever make real art. This has always been the thrill of teaching for me. In fact it has been something of a life mission.

Somewhere along the line, however, I started to become known as the "serious" teacher, the one who will break you down, old-school style. "Stay away from Rob, unless you are serious about this art business." I'm not really sure how this perception has been altered. My believe that art can and should be accessible to everyone has not changed.

Which brings us back to the question of how to explain the growing popularity of this drink and paint business model. They are successfully pulling in 30-40 people, day in and day out, painting away, usually a very simple, not always very compelling graphic image. No commitment, just a one-time fling. It reminds me a little of the Bill Alexander method (Bob Ross's predecessor), who famously quipped, "I teach people how to make a painting you might pay $25 for at a garage sale," There is little being offered in the way of method, inquiry or individual intention; it is simply rote painting. Everyone is painting the same thing at the same time. The host reassures you, "just do what I do and no one will be disappointed." You are guaranteed to go home with pretty much the same painting as the friend who dared you to come, all with the aid of a few stiff drinks to chase the intimidating art goblins away. I think the key to success for this model is that they have virtually eliminated the risk of failure.

It is a breakdown in my marketing that potential students fear having to confront the possibility of failure in my classes. Although I do agree the only way to do anything extraordinary in the creative realm is to risk failure. My quaint solution to this dilemma has been to neutralize ego, which is the part of us that registers whether something we do is a success or a failure. Picasso himself said it best, "I leave my ego at the door when I paint." In my classes I focus on creating an inspiring space to explore and see and try new things in a safe, *critic-free* environment where the shear joy of self-expression can flourish.

So who are all these not-so-serious, wine drinking art spirits and why aren't they painting with me? After all, aren't these the same people I have been working miracles with over the last thirty years? My father used to say, "there is the right way to do something, and then there is the easy way." I sincerely believe, perhaps naively, that with a little concrete method to back us up we humans are capable of much more than we might otherwise believe ourselves capable. I say, "teach a man to fish, rather than show him how to paint this particular fish." Not that I am in any way discouraging people from enjoying the experience of a fun night of painting while intoxicated. There is a lovely social element that is very gratifying. And I'm always in favor of any excuse to throw some paint around. But without the risk of failure, however slight I can make it, I suspect perhaps the possibility of accomplishment might be missing from the experience.

Now, I will tell you I have on occasion painted under the influence. But I tend to avoid using drugs and alcohol while creating for a number of reasons. One being, I'm afraid I will come to depend on the feeling of being uninhibited. I say feeling because that's what it is. I am under the influence of something external to me, an altered state. This altered state often feels heightened. But is it truly heightened, as in getting me closer to the truth deep inside me? This leads to the question of whether my getting to the truth is required for me to have a fun artsy experience.

In all fairness to famous geniuses like Richard Burton and Jim Morrison, who used drugs and alcohol to great affect, I have to admit that in my experience I have sometimes received a glimpse of something true that I could not see while sober. But in the process I have noticed I am also giving up something else that is equally important: a certain clarity of vision that makes the idea powerful and coherent. I have discovered (and shared) over the years a number of mind tricks that create a similar sense of altered reality without the use of external stimulants.

So what's the upshot of all this? I say do whatever you need to do to get to the place where you are self-expressed, where you are enjoying your God-given right to explore the joy of creation. Hopefully, these wine drinking painting orgies are a gateway for more people to discover their creative selves. But whatever you do, may you find a new way to do it, a way you'd never thought was practical, a way that brings you closer to the joy of connecting to the endless universe of possibilities.

End

www.ingramcontent.com/pod-product-compliance
Lightning Source LLC
Chambersburg PA
CBHW051504170526
45166CB00001B/374

* 9 781478 123545 *